SCHOLASTIC

ACTIVE Grammar

Practice Book 3

Rosemary Allen

Name ____________________

Class ____________________

AF530508

Previously published as Grammar Skills 3 by Learners Publishing Pte Ltd.

First edition 2012
Reprinted 2012, 2013, 2014 (thrice), 2015 (twice), 2016, 2017, 2018, 2019, 2020, 2023, 2024, 2025

ISBN 978-81-8477-748-2

CONTENTS

 ISBN 978-81-8477-748-2

To Teachers and Parents

The study of English grammar in schools is changing as educators become increasingly aware of the important role context plays in language learning. The functional use of grammar has become a feature of English syllabuses around the world.

Active Grammar Practice Books have been written specifically to provide students with valuable links between basic, traditional grammatical concepts and the functional contexts in which they are used. The activities represent a blend of traditional and functional approaches to describe how texts 'work' in real-life situations and why certain grammatical choices are considered appropriate. Traditional grammar serves to provide students with the special terminology needed to talk about grammar, while functional grammar is intended to improve communicative competence by showing students how grammar works in the context of different text types.

The exercises in this book give students systematic guidance in developing an understanding of grammatical concepts. Throughout the books there are panel notes that give hints for correct usage and highlight exceptions to grammar rules, as well as provide simple non-technical definitions to help students understand the exercises. Many of the exercises incorporate learner-centred activities that include completing rhymes and short stories, solving riddles and puzzles, doing word searches and seeing 'language-in-action'. At the same time, the activities provide teachers with a range of techniques to use, techniques that have proven highly successful with both native and non-native speakers of English. The exercises are graded, but include challenging ones to motivate as well as interest the students.

It is hoped that teachers will find this series a valuable tool in their teaching programme, one that will provide young learners with a fascinating journey into the world of English language and a sound knowledge of how it works.

 ISBN 978-81-8477-748-2

1 Articles

A Read the story below and circle all the articles that you can find.

Once there was a small boy who lived in an igloo in the North Pole. One day, when it was snowing heavily outside, the boy became very bored staying in the igloo. Without asking permission, the boy took his father's long spear, an axe and a fishing pole. "I am going to catch a fish for dinner," he thought.

The axe was very sharp and soon the boy had cut a hole in the ice. He was so busy fishing that he did not notice a polar bear lurking close by. The bear had a white coat, so the boy was unable to see it. Closer and closer, the bear padded towards the small boy, until it was so close that only a metre separated them.

> **Did You Know?**
>
> You use the indefinite articles **a** and **an** when you mention something for the first time. If you refer to it again, you often use the definite article **the.**
>
> The definite article is also used when you are referring to a particular one, such as **the** National Library.

Suddenly, the boy heard an enormous shout. He looked up and saw his father frantically waving an oar at the bear. The shout made the bear panic and it ran hurriedly away across the slippery ice. The oar had frightened it.

"You nearly became the bear's dinner, my son!" scolded his father. "Next time you must tell me when you want to go fishing. We will go together."

 ISBN 978-81-8477-748-2

B *Fill in **a** or **an** in the blanks to complete the two poems.*

Homes

I live in ______ apartment.

My friend lives in ______ house.

An Eskimo lives in ______ igloo,

But ______ hole is the home for ______ mouse.

Pets

May has ______ cute pet rabbit.

John has ______ angora cat.

Joy has ______ curly poodle,

But I have ______ big white rat.

May feeds her rabbit ______ apple a day,

John gives his cat ______ fish.

Joy buys her poodle ______ ice cream,

But my rat likes ______ cookie in his dish.

 ISBN 978-81-8477-748-2

C Add a, an or the to complete these sentences.

1. We went for ______ boat ride down ______ Singapore River.
2. Many people like to shop at ______ supermarket near ______ station.
3. The workers are building ______ underground railway to link ______ two main towns.
4. ______ two boys wanted to buy ______ ice cream, but ______ corner store was shut.
5. ______ eerie sound was heard as we entered. ______ sound seemed to have come from nowhere.
6. When we were leaving ______ school hall, all of ______ lights suddenly went out, and I tripped over ______ chair.

D Fill in the blanks with suitable articles. Put a X in the blank if the sentence does not require an article. The first two are done for you.

It was __the__ school holidays and Mum was preparing __X__ breakfast. First she turned on ______ tap to fill ______ kettle. Then she asked ______ children, "What would you like for breakfast, ______ children?"

Jane replied, "I'd like ______ toast and ______ cheese and ______ cup of hot chocolate."

Did You Know

Uncountable nouns do not need articles. **Plural nouns** only need **the** if the listener knows which things or people you mean. **A** and **an** are only used with **singular countable nouns**. Look at page 10 to find out more about this.

Richard replied, "I'd like ______ apple pie and ______ glass of milk."

Nora said, "I'd really love ______ French fries. But I don't like ______ milk to drink, so I'll have ______ hot chocolate also."

Dad looked at Mum and grinned. "I think ______ children want to go to ______ hamburger shop down ______ road. Turn off ______ kettle and let's have ______ treat today!"

 ISBN 978-81-8477-748-2

E Fill in the blanks with suitable articles to complete the story.

The Man and His Two Daughters

There was once ______ man who had two daughters. They were married on ______ same day. He married ______ elder daughter to ______ gardener and ______ younger daughter to ______ potter.

A few weeks after the wedding, he went to visit ______ two families. First he visited ______ gardener's house, and he asked his elder daughter how things were going. "Fine," she said. "Things are going well, and I am happy. But ______ weather is too dry. ______ soil needs more rain so that ______ plants can grow strong and tall."

Then he visited ______ potter's house, and asked his younger daughter how things were going.

"Fine," she said. "Things are going well, and I am happy. But ______ weather is too wet. We need more sun so that ______ pottery will dry quickly in ______ heat."

"Oh dear," said ______ man as he returned to his own house. "I was going to ask ______ gods to grant ______ girls whatever they desired, but now I had better say nothing."

 ISBN 978-81-8477-748-2

2 Common Nouns

A *Here's a mixed bag of words. They are all common nouns. Can you group them correctly according to the headings below?*

clown	dolphin	astronaut	monkey
park	amphibian	theatre	book
robot	scarecrow	dinosaur	apron
gym	twins	acrobat	field

Did You Know?

Nouns are words for people, things, places or animals. For example, **cat**, **dog**, **snake** … are words for animals; **artist**, **lawyer**, **teacher** … are words for people; **mat**, **pen**, **ruler** … are words for things; and **bank**, **playground**, **river** … are words for places.

People

1. ______________
2. ______________
3. ______________
4. ______________

Places

1. ______________
2. ______________
3. ______________
4. ______________

Animals

1. ______________
2. ______________
3. ______________
4. ______________

Things

1. ______________
2. ______________
3. ______________
4. ______________

 ISBN 978-81-8477-748-2

B ***Underline the nouns in the sentences below.***

1. My grandad bought me a present yesterday.
2. The woman is reading a book.
3. The man is mowing the lawn.
4. These chairs and desks are damaged.
5. The farmers are harvesting their crops.
6. A lot of people got off at the station.
7. He found two treasure chests in the cave.
8. Young children are good at using the computer.
9. The stepmother was very angry with her stepdaughter.
10. All the workmen are working very hard to complete the building.
11. There was very little rain last month.
12. The king and the queen lived in a palace.
13. Let's go for a walk along the beach.
14. The rooster is crowing.
15. The lioness is chasing her prey.

 ISBN 978-81-8477-748-2

C *Sort the nouns in the box into **countable** or **uncountable nouns.** Then write the **plural** form for each of the countable nouns.*

snow	island	sandwich	tea
valley	work	plastic	toast
shape	milk	spaceman	diary
dust	echo	furniture	scarf
bread	air	mouse	half

Did You Know

Countable nouns are words for things that can be counted. Countable nouns can be **singular** or **plural**.

Uncountable nouns are words for things that can't be counted.

Uncountable Noun
______
______
______
______
______
______
______
______
______
______

Countable Noun	Plural
______	______
______	______
______	______
______	______
______	______
______	______
______	______
______	______
______	______
______	______

 ISBN 978-81-8477-748-2

D ***Find the nouns for eight musical instruments from the word box. Put a circle round each of them.***

K	P	T	A	M	C										
R	I	E	R	Y	P										
E	A	W	H	I	T										
F	N	E	C	O	A	S	H	C	A	X					
T	O	N	X	V	I	N	O	E	D	Z					
Y	O	H	A	R	P	U	G	L	Q	V					
					T	W	F	L	U	T	E	P	D	W	I
					P	R	X	O	E	A	L	R	I	J	E
					F	E	J	Y	T	R	U	M	P	E	T
										M	H	A	B	Y	E
										V	I	O	L	I	N
										E	M	Y	E	L	T

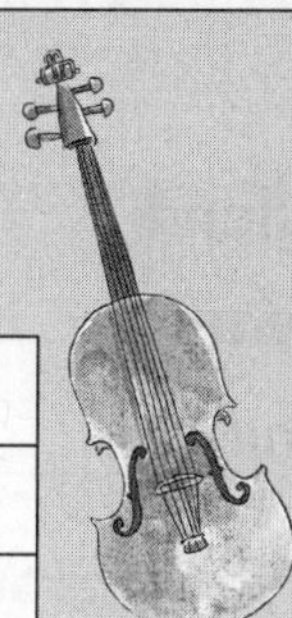

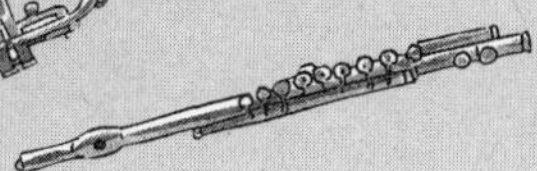
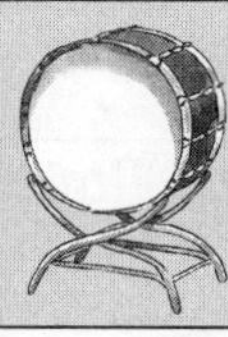

Write the eight musical instruments in the spaces below.

Write the plural form after each musical instrument.

1. ____________________ ____________________
2. ____________________ ____________________
3. ____________________ ____________________
4. ____________________ ____________________
5. ____________________ ____________________
6. ____________________ ____________________
7. ____________________ ____________________
8. ____________________ ____________________

 ISBN 978-81-8477-748-2

3 Proper Nouns

A Write the names of the following, using **proper nouns**.

1. the street where you live ______
2. your best friend ______
3. your teacher ______
4. the title of your favourite book ______
5. a special building or monument ______
6. a festival ______
7. a river ______
8. a mountain ______

Did You Know

Special names given to people, things, places, roads, mountains, festivals and books are called **proper nouns**. They always begin with capital letters.

B Rewrite the titles of these books or films, using capital letters where necessary.

1. the adventures of tom sawyer ______
2. the wolf and the seven little kids ______
3. the golden goose ______
4. harry potter and the chamber of secrets ______
5. little red riding hood ______
6. home alone ______
7. jurassic park ______
8. my first science dictionary ______

 ISBN 978-81-8477-748-2

C *Underline the **proper nouns** in the following sentences, then rewrite the sentences correctly.*

1. The guests stayed in the royal hotel in green st.

2. We are going to climb mount faber tomorrow.

3. Janet is reading the story of peter pan.

4. Lots of visitors like to go to orchard road for shopping.

5. Those students go to thames public school in london.

6. Christmas falls on the 25th of december.

7. The explorers reached the south pole in june.

8. The brazilians are very good football players.

9. My mother bought some french perfume in paris.

10. Dad said john could go to the star cinema on wednesday with david.

 ISBN 978-81-8477-748-2

D *Look at the picture. The places numbered 1—8 have not been named. Make up a* ***proper noun*** *for each of these places as shown in the example for the theatre. Don't forget to use capital letters in the names.*

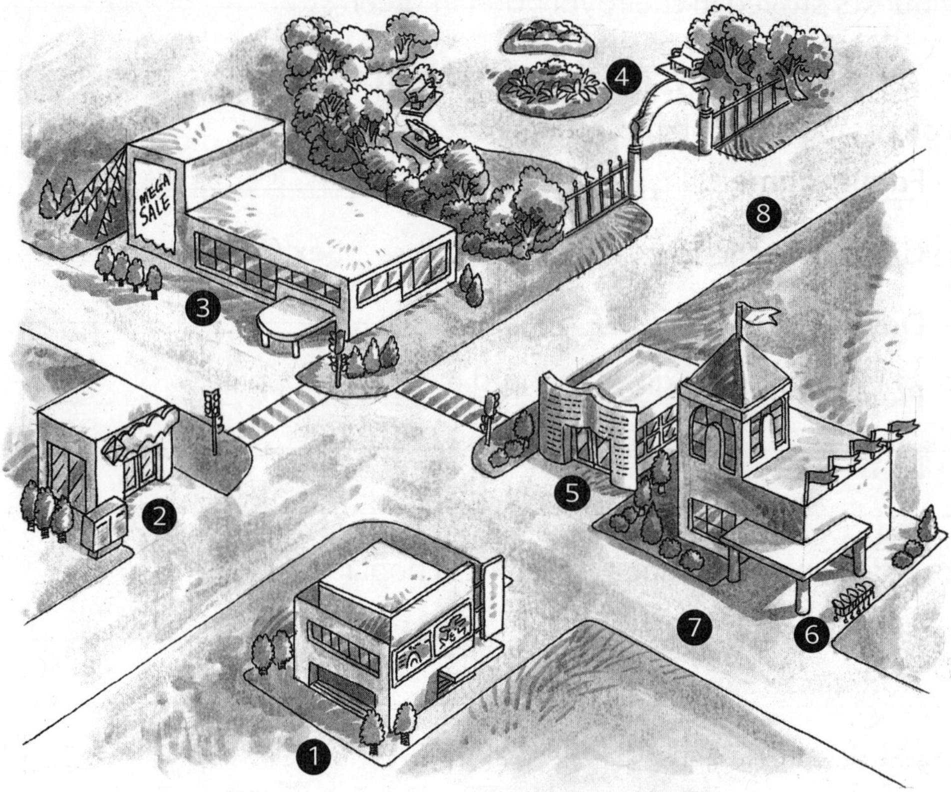

1. The theatre: Regal Theatre
2. The post office ______
3. The department store ______
4. The park ______
5. The book store ______
6. The supermarket ______

The two streets:

7. ______
8. ______

 ISBN 978-81-8477-748-2

E *You and your parents are flying to Hong Kong on holiday. Before the plane lands, fill in this landing card.*

Disembarkation Card

Family name ______________________________

Given name ________________ Sex (M/F) ________

Date of birth ______________________________

Place of birth ______________________________

Nationality ______________________________

Passport No. ______________________________

Issued in ______________________________

Address in Hong Kong Friendly Hotel, Kowloon

Home address ______________________________

____

____

_ _ _ _ _ _ _ _ _ _ _ _ _ _   _ _ _ _ _ _ _ _ _

Signature   *Date*

 ISBN 978-81-8477-748-2

4 Other Types of Nouns

A *Fill in the missing* ***masculine*** *and* ***feminine nouns*** *to complete the following story. Then find all the masculine and feminine nouns in the story and write them in the correct boxes below.*

A Royal Party

The princess stamped her feet angrily. Her mother, the ____________, and her father, the ____________, had sent invitations to her birthday party to males only and not to ____________. Her mother had invited the lords but not the ____________, the dukes but not the ____________, the counts but not the ____________. Her brother, the ____________, had asked a wizard but not a ____________ and a lad from the village, but not a ____________.

"Whatever were you thinking? You will have to send new invitations. I want ____________ as well as men at my party," she demanded.

The new invitations were sent and the guests all had a good time.

Did You Know

Words for boys, men and male animals are called **masculine nouns**. Words for girls, women and female animals are called **feminine nouns**. Words that can be used for both males and females are called **common-gender nouns**.

Masculine Nouns	Feminine Nouns

Can you find one common-gender noun in the story?

Write it in this space. ____________

 ISBN 978-81-8477-748-2

B *The following are words for people and animals. Sort them according to either **masculine** or **feminine** or **common-gender nouns** and write them in the correct boxes.*

leopardess	cattle	vixen	buck	mouse	ram
drake	mare	housemaid	landlord	pupil	niece
butler	engineer	matron	cousin	president	monk

Feminine Nouns	Masculine Nouns	Common-gender Nouns
______	______	______
______	______	______
______	______	______
______	______	______
______	______	______
______	______	______

C *Write 5 sentences using each pair of masculine and feminine nouns in the same sentence.*

1. ____

____ (uncle, aunt)

2. ____

____ (cock, hen)

3. ____

____ (ladies, gentlemen)

4. ____

____ (boy, girl)

5. ____

____ (husband, wife)

 ISBN 978-81-8477-748-2

D

The words in the box are used as* collective nouns *for groups of people. Write the correct collective noun for each picture.

an audience	a crew
an orchestra	a class
a choir	a team
a family	a committee

Did You Know?

Collective nouns are words for groups of people, animals and things.

1. ______________________

2. ______________________

3. ______________________

4. ______________________

5. ______________________

6. ______________________

7. ______________________

8. ______________________

 ISBN 978-81-8477-748-2

E *The words below are used as collective nouns for groups of animals or things. Can you think of nouns that go with them? Write them in the blanks.*

1. a fleet of ____________
2. a litter of ____________
3. a bouquet of ____________
4. a pride of ____________
5. a herd of ____________
6. a swarm of ____________
7. a flight of ____________
8. a bunch of ____________
9. a comb of ____________
10. a shoal of ____________

F *Can you think of suitable collective nouns for the following groups of animals and things? Write them in the blanks. Remember to add* ***a*** *or* ***an*** *before the collective noun.*

1. a pile of newspapers
2. ____________ of beads
3. ____________ of trees
4. ____________ of flats
5. ____________ of ants
6. ____________ of birds
7. ____________ of wolves
8. ____________ of cubs

 ISBN 978-81-8477-748-2

5 Personal Pronouns

A *Fill in the blanks with suitable **pronouns** that refer to the nouns in bold print.*

1. **The car** broke down.
   __________ broke down.
2. **Sam** saw a snake.
   __________ saw a snake.
3. **The dogs** are fighting again.
   __________ are fighting again.

> **Did You Know**
>
> **Pronouns** take the place of common nouns and proper nouns.
>
> You use the **personal pronouns: I, you, he, she, it, we, they** as a subject.
>
> You use the **personal pronouns: me, you, him, her, it, us, them** as an object.

4. **The girls** dressed beautifully for the party.
   __________ dressed beautifully for the party.
5. **The train** will leave in ten minutes.
   __________ will leave in ten minutes.
6. **Robert and I** cycled along the path by the sea.
   __________ cycled along the path by the sea.

7. Alice's mother asked **Alice** to buy some sugar.
   Alice's mother asked __________ to buy some sugar.
8. Peter's father asked **Peter** to buy a newspaper.
   Peter's father asked __________ to buy a newspaper.
9. I am typing a letter for **Susan**.
   I am typing a letter for __________.

10. The teacher is teaching **the children** how to swim.
    The teacher is teaching __________ how to swim.

 ISBN 978-81-8477-748-2

B Fill in the blanks with suitable pronouns.

she	they	he	it	we	you

1. Josephine liked the dress. __________ paid $30 for it.
2. Jeff came to my house. __________ went for a swim together.
3. Sue has seen the movie twice and says __________ is very exciting.
4. The twins often quarrel. Sometimes __________ even fight.
5. "Are __________ ill?" Miss Lee asked Kate.
6. Ben could not understand the sum. __________ asked Miss Lee to explain to him one more time.

C Fill in the blanks with suitable pronouns.

it	me	him	them	you	us	her

1. John, here is a book for __________.
2. Sue and I are classmates. I sit next to __________.
3. We were noisy. The teacher scolded __________.
4. Where's my key? I can't find __________.
5. "Are you coming with __________, Janet?" asked Lily.
6. James and Peter asked me to play with __________.
7. It's not my fault. Don't blame __________.
8. The police caught the man and took __________ to the police station.

 ISBN 978-81-8477-748-2

D *Use suitable **pronouns** to complete the story.*

they them he she I us we it you me

Holiday Plans

The children were sharing their holiday plans with their teacher, Miss Lee. __________ asked __________ where __________ were going for their holiday.

"Well, my Mum wants to go to Australia because __________ wants to see the kangaroos and koalas, but my Dad doesn't like the idea. __________ wants to go to Penang and enjoy the beach," said Tom. "So __________ don't know where __________ will go."

"My cousins went to Australia last year and stayed on a farm. __________ showed __________ their photos. There was a pet calf on the farm and __________ were allowed to feed __________," said Grace.

"I think the farm is the place for my brothers and __________," decided Lisa. "__________ must try to persuade Dad to take __________ there instead of the mountains where __________ were planning to go."

"Where are __________ going, Miss Lee?" asked the children.

"__________ am going to stay home and rest! This has been a busy year and __________ need it," replied Miss Lee.

 ISBN 978-81-8477-748-2

E ***What are the nouns referred to by the pronouns in bold print in the following sentences? Write the nouns in the space provided. The first one is done for you.***

1. Squirrels have long claws. **They** can cling to trees. — 1. Squirrels
2. The Eiffel Tower is a famous building. **It** took two years to build. — 2. ____________
3. The Taj Mahal was built by an Indian emperor. **He** built **it** to remember his wife. — 3. ____________ ____________
4. Dad and I cycled to the seaside. **We** went there to fish. — 4. ____________
5. Your shoes are dirty. Go and wash **them**. — 5. ____________
6. Granny was ill. Mum went to visit **her**. — 6. ____________
7. Here are Paul and Peter. **They** are my brothers. — 7. ____________
8. Hi, Alice! How are **you**? — 8. ____________
9. The hare challenged the tortoise to a race. **He** agreed. — 9. ____________
10. The wind was very strong. **It** uprooted some trees. — 10. ____________
11. My name is Peter. **I** am ten. — 11. ____________
12. Johnson, Sue and I often go the playground. **We** play football there. — 12. ____________
13. There are plenty of computers in our school. We use **them** for our lessons. — 13. ____________
14. This computer is too slow. We have to change **it**. — 14. ____________

 ISBN 978-81-8477-748-2

6 More Pronouns: Demonstrative, Reflexive, Possessive

A *Write what you think each speaker is saying. Use **these, this, that** or **those** in your answers. Also, use the keywords in the speech bubbles to help you.*

Did You Know

When **this, that, these** and **those** are used to take the place of nouns, they are called **demonstrative pronouns.**

You use **this** and **these** for people or things that are close to you. You use **that** or **those** for people or things that are further away.

 ISBN 978-81-8477-748-2

puppy dog

3. ____

____

____

python tiger

4. ____

____

____

caterpillar butterfly

5. ____

____

____

 ISBN 978-81-8477-748-2

B *Fill in the blanks with suitable* ***reflexive pronouns.***

ourselves	herself	myself	themselves
yourself	itself	himself	yourselves

Did You Know

Reflexive pronouns are words like **myself**, **himself**, **herself**. They refer back to the subject of the sentence.

Reflexive pronouns can be used to emphasize something about the subject.

1. We built the hut ________________.
2. Catherine made the dress ________________.
3. All the children enjoyed ________________ on Christmas.
4. I wrote the poem ________________.
5. Don't blame other people for your mistake.

   Blame ________________.
6. He fell off the chair and hurt ________________.
7. "Children, behave ________________," commanded the scout leader.
8. We must learn to protect ________________.
9. The old woman lived all by ________________.
10. The baby bird is too young to look for food ________________.
11. Our teacher wants us to introduce ________________ to the guests.
12. How does the chameleon protect ________________ from its enemies?
13. He is pleased with ________________.
14. We will complete the job ________________.
15. Paul, do it ________________!

 ISBN 978-81-8477-748-2

C Read this short play. Underline the **possessive pronouns** and circle the **possessive adjectives**.

Mrs Han told her children to clean up their rooms. The children are arguing.

Mary: Those shoes are yours, May. I'm not putting your shoes away. I'll put mine away, but you can take yours with you.

May: OK, I'll put my own shoes away, but I'll have to put them in your shoe cupboard because mine is full.

Tom: These CD-Roms are not mine. Are they yours, May?

May: Yes, they're mine.

Tom: Here're some tennis racquets. Are they ours? Jane and Francis said they left theirs here yesterday.

Mary: No, they're our racquets. Mum put theirs in the hall cupboard so that they wouldn't get mixed up with ours.

May: Well, my part of the room looks better. Look at Mary's. Hers is still a bit messy. How is yours, Tom?

Tom: Mine is looking much better. I think Mum will be pleased.

Did You Know

- The words **mine, ours, yours, his, hers** and **theirs** are called **possessive pronouns**. You use them to say who something belongs to.
- **Possessive adjectives** are **my, our, your, his, her, its, their**. You use these words before nouns to say who something belongs to.

D Rewrite these sentences, using the **possessive pronouns**. The first one is done for you.

1. This is Mike's drink. This drink is his.
2. These are my pyjamas. These pyjamas are ________.
3. This is Jane's apron. This apron is ________.
4. That is Mr Lee's medicine. That medicine is ________.
5. These are your stamps. These stamps are ________.
6. This is Sue and Tom's pet. This pet is ________.
7. This is our flat. This flat is ________.

 ISBN 978-81-8477-748-2

E *The pictures below show some pets and their owners. Write the labels at the bottom of each picture, using* ***apostrophes*** *to show who owns each animal. The first one is done for you.*

1. Mandy's cat

4. ______________________

2. ______________________

5. ______________________

3. ______________________

6. ______________________

Did You Know

You use an **apostrophe** (') to show who owns something.

When the noun is **singular**, the apostrophe comes **before** the **s**. When a singular noun or name (e.g. **James**) ends in **–s**, you add an apostrophe in the usual way, then another **s**: **James's** toys.

When the noun is **plural**, you put the apostrophe **after** the **–s**.

F *Change the following sentences, using* ***apostrophes*** *to show ownership.*

1. These dolls belong to Jill. These are ______________ dolls.
2. This sharpener belongs to Joe. This is ______________ sharpener.
3. That car belongs to Miss Lee. That is ______________ car.
4. This orchard belongs to Uncle Jim. This is ______________ orchard.
5. That backpack belongs to Peter. That is ______________ backpack.

 ISBN 978-81-8477-748-2

7 Adjectives

A *Read the poem below and underline the **adjectives** in it.*

Did You Know?

Adjectives are describing words. You use them to describe people, places or things.

Adjectives usually come **before** the noun they describe, but sometimes they can come **after** the noun they describe, later in the sentence.

Airport

Many visitors enter my buildings.
Some are tired, some are nervous, some are sad,
Some are excited or eager or frightened,
Others are happy, contented and glad.

There are doorways for departing passengers,
And doorways for those inward-bound.
There are customs officers and pilots,
And tropical plants all around.

 ISBN 978-81-8477-748-2

B *Circle the most suitable **adjective** in the brackets for each sentence.*

1. We saw a (**green / huge / comical**) elephant at the zoo.
2. He helped the (**happy / open / injured**) cyclist to his feet.
3. She heard a (**hard / strange / rich**) sound during the night.
4. Her (**torn / new / empty**) dress was soon repaired.
5. The students couldn't solve the (**easy / friendly / difficult**) problem.
6. His gift was a (**lonely / pleasant / narrow**) surprise for Julie.
7. The (**sharp / blunt / clever**) knife sliced through the cheese.
8. The (**invisible / rare / loud**) coin had become very valuable.
9. Some players were upset by the (**friendly / huge / hostile**) crowd.
10. Peter heard a (**loud / distant / noisy**) cry which was very faint.

Did You Know

Many nouns can be changed to adjectives by adding these endings: **-y**, **-al**, **-ful**, **-less**, **-able**, **-ish**, **-ous**.

C *Some **adjectives** are formed from nouns. Change these nouns to adjectives. The first one is done for you.*

1. harm	harmful	7. love	______
2. dust	______	8. grace	______
3. nation	______	9. music	______
4. home	______	10. juice	______
5. child	______	11. fool	______
6. danger	______	12. comfort	______

 ISBN 978-81-8477-748-2

D ***The words in the box can be used as adjectives. Choose the correct adjective to complete each sentence.***

interesting	barking	bearded	crowded
living	frightening	used	stolen
gifted	broken	working	describing

Did You Know

Some **present participles** (verbs ending in **-ing**) and **past participles** (verbs ending in **-ed, -en**) can be used as adjectives.

1. Plants are ________________ things.
2. The ________________ hours of most companies are from 9:00 am to 5:00 pm.
3. The timid girl doesn't like ________________ places.
4. They had a ________________ experience last night.
5. A ________________ dog is very annoying.
6. An adjective is a ________________ word.
7. The ________________ man is wanted by the police.
8. The ________________ child played the violin superbly.
9. Don't sit on the ________________ chair.
10. The thief tried to sell the ________________ watches.
11. I can only afford to buy a ________________ car.
12. This looks like an ________________ movie.

 ISBN 978-81-8477-748-2

E ***Underline the adjectives in these sentences.***
In the blanks, write the noun described by each adjective.

1. Everyone wished James a happy birthday. ____________
2. Greek is a difficult language. ____________
3. The teacher is holding a thick book. ____________
4. The residents heard a loud explosion. ____________
5. The giant lived in a beautiful garden. ____________
6. I like colourful dresses. ____________
7. All the pupils have the correct answer. ____________
8. I have a special gift for you. ____________

F ***Can you think of a suitable adjective that has the same meaning as the one in bold print? Write your answers in the blanks.***

1. The little girl is wearing a **beautiful** dress. ____________
2. It is a **nice** day. ____________
3. I hope you have a **good** journey. ____________
4. The witch was a **bad** woman. ____________
5. The soldiers were **brave**. ____________
6. John always takes the **largest** share. ____________
7. These new computers are very **expensive**. ____________
8. What a **strange** person he is! ____________

 ISBN 978-81-8477-748-2

8 Adjectives That Compare

A ***Read the following story about Mrs Park's children. The words in bold are the comparative or superlative forms of adjectives. Write an opposite above each of these adjectives.***

Mrs Park had triplets, but they were very different from each other. Jenny and Jane looked alike, but Jenny was **lighter** than Jane and **shorter**. She was also **more athletic**. Janet was the **smallest** of the three. She was also the **cleverest** and won the **most** prizes at school. Jane was a **faster** runner than Janet, but **slower** than Jenny. However, the triplets were alike in one way — they were the **best** readers in school. They borrowed **more** books than anyone else in their class. This made their mother the **happiest** parent in town.

B ***What are the* comparative *and* superlative *forms of these adjectives?***

	Positive	Comparative	Superlative
1.	fit	fitter	fittest
2.	graceful		
3.	delicious		
4.	narrow		
5.	dangerous		
6.	naughty		
7.	attractive		
8.	funny		

Did You Know?

You use a **comparative adjective** to compare two things. When you are comparing more than two things, you use a **superlative adjective**.

When an adjective has more than one syllable you often use the words **more** and **most** before the adjective.

 ISBN 978-81-8477-748-2

C Fill the blanks using the comparative or superlative form of the adjective in brackets.

1. A plane is ____________ than a helicopter. (**fast**)
2. Mirror, mirror, on the wall, who is the ____________ of us all? (**pretty**)
3. Winter is the ____________ season of the year. (**cold**)
4. This is the ____________ pumpkin I have ever seen. (**big**)
5. Today is ____________ than yesterday. (**sunny**)

6. This is our ____________ computer. (**good**)
7. Ahmad is ____________ than Ali. (**strong**)
8. My brother is two years ____________ than me. (**young**)

D Choose the correct colour words from the box to complete the comparison.

red	blue	pink	brown	black	white	green	yellow

1. as ____________ as coal
2. as ____________ as snow
3. as ____________ as blood
4. as ____________ as the sky
5. as ____________ as a berry
6. as ____________ as grass
7. as ____________ as a flamingo
8. as ____________ as a sunflower

 ISBN 978-81-8477-748-2

E ***The table below compares the age, height and weight of five children. Fill in the blanks using the correct form of the adjective in brackets.***

	Paul	**Sue**	**Peter**	**John**	**Lisa**
age	9 yrs old	8 yrs old	10 yrs old	7 yrs old	6 yrs old
height	137 cm	130 cm	135 cm	130 cm	128 cm
weight	32 kg	28 kg	35 kg	30 kg	26 kg

1. Peter is the ________________ of the children. (**old**)
2. Lisa is the ________________ of the children. (**young**)
3. Paul is the ________________ of all. (**tall**)
4. John is not as ________________ as Sue. (**old**)
5. Lisa is ________________ than John and Sue. (**short**)
6. Peter is the ________________ in the group. (**heavy**)
7. John is ________________ than Lisa. (**tall**)
8. Sue is ________________ than John. (**light**)
9. Sue is ________________ than Lisa, but ________________ than Peter. (**old, young**)
10. John is ________________ than Peter, but ________________ than Sue. (**light, heavy**)

 ISBN 978-81-8477-748-2

F Match an animal to the most suitable **adjective.**

Adjectives			Animals
slow	•	•	mouse
cunning	•	•	mule
big	•	•	lion
brave	•	•	ox
timid	•	•	eel
strong	•	•	snail
slippery	•	•	whale
stubborn	•	•	fox

G Complete these sentences using the matching adjective and animal in Exercise F to complete the **comparative form as ... as.** The first one is done for you.

1. If you want the job done, don't ask James. He's as slow as a snail.
2. Watch out! She's sure to trick you. She's as ____________________.
3. If you're frightened, take Kim with you. She's as ____________________.
4. That log is heavy. Tom will help you. He's as ____________________.
5. She won't co-operate because she's as ____________________.
6. You eat far too much. You'll soon be as ____________________.
7. You'll have to hold the vase tightly. It's as ____________________.
8. Lisa won't sing at the concert. She's as ____________________.

 ISBN 978-81-8477-748-2

9 Determiners

A ***Read the conversation below and underline the quantifying determiners.***

> **Did You Know**
>
> Some words tell you how many people or things there are without giving you the exact number or quantity, like **some, several, much, many, a few, lots of, plenty.** These words are called **quantifying determiners.** They are also called **quantifiers.** Many of them are used with **of.**

Mrs Han needed to bake some cakes, so her two children May and Tom went to the store to buy the ingredients for their mother.

Grocer: Hello children, what can I do for you today?

May: We need to buy some flour, some sugar, some butter, lots of eggs and plenty of chocolate bits. Mum is going to make several cakes because we're going to have a party tomorrow.

Grocer: Well, how much of each ingredient do you need? How many eggs do you want — how much sugar and flour, how much butter?

Tom: Mum said ten eggs. She asked us to buy one kilogram bag of sugar.

May: We need two tubs of butter and three packets of chocolate bits.

Tom: And a kilogram bag of flour.

Grocer: Here are all the things you've ordered and here are two lollipops for each of you for being such good children. I hope you'll have lots of fun at your party.

May & Tom: Thanks. We'll save you a few cakes.

B ***Write much or many to complete these sentences.***

> **Did You Know**
>
> You use **many** with countable nouns, and **much** with uncountable nouns.

1. How ____________ orange juice is left?
2. How ____________ legs does an octopus have?
3. There isn't ____________ food in the fridge.
4. Is there ____________ time left before the game is over?
5. How ____________ times must I tell you?
6. Mum didn't add ____________ items to the shopping list.

 ISBN 978-81-8477-748-2

C *Use **some** or **any** to complete the sentences below.*

1. Are there ____________ letters for me?
2. Here are ____________ letters for you.
3. Do you have ____________ problems with your new computer?
4. I don't want ____________ apples.
5. I would like ____________ more tea, please.
6. Did ____________ of you complete the exercise?
7. I can't find ____________ paper in the house.
8. ____________ plants don't need much water to live.

Did You Know

You can use **some** and **any** with **countable nouns** or **uncountable nouns.**

You use **any** after **not** and other **negative** words, as well as in questions.

You use **some** in questions where the answer **yes** is expected, as well as in offers and requests.

D *Look at the pictures. Use **some** or **any** to complete your answers to the following questions.*

1. Is there any ice cream left in the tub?

Yes, there is some.

No, there isn't any left in the tub.

2. Are there any shirts with stripes?

Yes, ____________

No, ____________

3. Are there any girls in the queue?

Yes, ____________

No, ____________

4. Are there any cakes on the plate?

Yes, ____________

No, ____________

 ISBN 978-81-8477-748-2

E Use *a few* or *a little* to complete the following sentences.

1. John has ________________ good friends.
2. Mr Yakub has a lot of watches.
   ________________ of them are very expensive.
3. Please add ________________ salt to the soup.
4. He has only ________________ coins.
5. I can see ________________ houses on the hill.
6. Take ________________ food before you go back to work.
7. There are only ________________ people in the queue.
8. Pour ________________ water into the dough to make it soft.
9. My dog has given birth to ________________ puppies.
10. The customers showed ________________ interest in the paintings.
11. Judy borrowed ________________ books from the library.
12. There is ________________ milk left for you.
13. I am playing football with ________________ friends.
14. The town has ________________ parks and playgrounds.
15. The boy is holding ________________ snow in his hands to make a snowball.

Did You Know

You use **a few** with **countable nouns**, and **a little** with **uncountable nouns**.

 ISBN 978-81-8477-748-2

F *Read the following passage and fill in the blanks with suitable* ***quantifying determiners*** *from the box.*

several	none	all	a few

Did You Know

The quantifying determiners **several**, **all** and **a few** can be followed by **of**, or used on their own as **pronouns**. **None** is always a pronoun and it can be followed by **of**.

A Damper of a Day

The day began very sunny. Only __________ clouds dotted the sky as the crowd moved towards the football ground. __________ people carried picnic baskets, but not __________ had brought umbrellas.

Before __________ the spectators could find their seats, the rain began to fall, without any warning. __________ spectators ran for shelter in the grandstand to watch the game that had just started. Although __________ of the fans would have chosen to stay in the rain to watch the game, not __________ could fit under the grandstand roof. So __________ weary fans were soaking wet.

The stand was almost empty by the end of the game because __________ people left before the game had finished. Only __________ people really enjoyed the game.

 ISBN 978-81-8477-748-2

10 Prepositions

A *Read the following limericks. Underline the 7* ***prepositions*** *that show place. Then circle the 6* ***prepositions*** *that show time.*

A girl **from** the Island of Jade
Was eating her lunch **in** the shade.
She sat **under** a tree
Beside the blue sea.
Then jumped **into** the water to wade.

Cinders entered the ballroom **at** eight,
She danced with the prince **until** late.
As the clock struck midnight
Her face turned pale white,
Cinders fled and jumped **over** the gate.

The Prince told the King in dismay
He must find his true love **before** May.
But the next day **at** 2:00,
Cinders tried on the shoe
And they wed **in** the church **on** that day.

Did You Know

Prepositions of place are small words that show **where** things happen.

Some prepositions show **when** things happen and they are called **prepositions of time.**

A **preposition** is always followed by a noun or pronoun.

 ISBN 978-81-8477-748-2

B *Use the prepositions of place and time in the box to complete the sentences. If the preposition in the sentence is used to show place, write **place** on the line after the sentence. If it is used to show time, write **time** on the line.*

to	beside	near	from
up	into	off	along
by	through	until	across

Did You Know?

You use **prepositions of place** to show not only place, but also position and direction.

You use **prepositions of time** to show time, or when something happens.

1. The ball rolled ___into___ a hole. — 1. ___place___
2. Starting __________ today, parking is not allowed in this area. — 2. __________
3. Miss Lee wants us to complete the project __________ next Monday. — 3. __________
4. Sue lives very __________ the school, so she walks __________ school every day. — 4. __________ __________
5. The people were not allowed to leave the building __________ they were told to do so. — 5. __________
6. Dad nearly fell __________ the ladder. — 6. __________
7. Sit __________ me so we can talk. — 7. __________
8. The dog ran __________ the pavement, then it dashed __________ the road. — 8. __________ __________
9. The cat squeezed __________ a gap in the fence. — 9. __________
10. We helped Uncle Ben push his car __________ the slope when it broke down. — 10. __________

 ISBN 978-81-8477-748-2

C Use a suitable **preposition** from the box to complete each sentence.

on	for	by	of	with

1. Come ___________ me to the beach.
2. Are you travelling ___________ train?
3. It is the third day ___________ June.
4. In olden times, people usually travelled from one place to another ___________ foot and ___________ horseback.
5. Miss Lee drew a big circle in the sand ___________ a stick.
6. Divide this box ___________ chocolates among yourselves.
7. You must apologize ___________ your rudeness.
8. The shirt ___________ blue stripes is too big ___________ me.
9. This palace was built ___________ the king specially ___________ his queen.
10. Mary always shares her toys ___________ her brother.

Did You Know

Many prepositions are used in special ways. For example, you can use:

- **by** and **on** to say how people and things travel;
- **by** and **with** to say how things are done or who does them;
- **with**, **of** and **for** to describe people, things and actions.

D Below is an invitation card which Susan has designed for her birthday party. Help her fill in the correct prepositions to complete the card.

 ISBN 978-81-8477-748-2

E *Fill in the blanks with suitable **prepositions**.*

1. We are all fond ____________ small animals.
2. My uncle lived ____________ a lake ____________ the forest.
3. The guests are all walking ____________ the stairs instead of waiting ____________ the lift.
4. The teacher took the toy gun ____________ the boy and locked it ____________ her desk.
5. The man was fined ____________ littering.
6. Keep ____________ the grass and walk only ____________ the path.
7. Can I go ____________ you ____________ the train station?
8. The boy dreamed ____________ an old man who gave him a magic brush.

F *The wrong prepositions are used in the sentences below. Draw a line through them and write the correct preposition in the box after the sentence.*

1. Come, sit besides me. [ ]
2. The girl was accused for stealing. [ ]
3. Look at the cartoon in page 20 of this magazine. [ ]
4. They finished the project by one week. [ ]
5. Can you lend your jacket from my friend? [ ]
6. How many continents are there on the world? [ ]
7. Mark was in the dentist's yesterday. [ ]
8. Tom always talks to his friends by the way to school. [ ]

 ISBN 978-81-8477-748-2

11 Adverbs and Adverbials

A *Change these adjectives into **adverbs**.*

Did You Know

You can form **adverbs** from some adjectives by adding **-ly** to them. Remember, if the adjective ends in **y**, you have to change **y** to **i** before adding **-ly**.

1. quiet ____________
2. correct ____________
3. angry ____________
4. cheerful ____________
5. enormous ____________
6. nice ____________
7. untidy ____________
8. polite ____________
9. rude ____________
10. happy ____________

B ***Some adjectives also end in -ly, like adverbs. Are the words in the list adjectives or adverbs? Put a tick in the correct box after each word. Then write a verb that can be used with each of the adverbs and a noun for each of the adjectives in the space provided.***

		Adverb	Adjective	
1.	friendly	☐	☐	____________
2.	heavily	☐	☐	____________
3.	closely	☐	☐	____________
4.	lovely	☐	☐	____________
5.	hurriedly	☐	☐	____________
6.	bravely	☐	☐	____________
7.	curly	☐	☐	____________
8.	ugly	☐	☐	____________

Remember

An **adverb** tells you more about a **verb** or an action, whereas an **adjective** describes a **noun**.

 ISBN 978-81-8477-748-2

C *Put a circle around each verb in the sentences and ask the question 'How?'. Then underline the* ***adverb of manner*** *which answers the question 'How?'. The first one is done for you.*

1. The door (opened) <u>suddenly</u>.
2. The jewels disappeared mysteriously.
3. Alice spoke calmly in front of her class.
4. She shouted at the man angrily.
5. We all studied hard for our exams.
6. The old man walked home slowly.
7. The boys divided the marbles equally among themselves.
8. The sun shone brightly.
9. The baby is sleeping soundly.
10. The washing dried quickly in the sun.
11. They all danced gracefully.
12. She packed hastily!
13. The hosts welcomed the guests warmly.
14. Everyone waited patiently for the bus.
15. I waved cheerfully to my neighbour.

Did You Know

Some adverbs tell you **how** the actions happen. They are called **adverbs of manner**. They describe verbs and answer the question 'How?'.

 ISBN 978-81-8477-748-2

D *Put a circle around the verb in each sentence and ask the question 'When?'. Underline the **adverb of time** which answers the question 'When?'.*

1. Please finish your work today.
2. We visited the orphanage yesterday.
3. They will start the project tomorrow.
4. Tim handed in his homework late.
5. Jill arrived early.
6. I must leave now.
7. They were at the same school last year.
8. I'll talk to you later.
9. Hurry, the bus is leaving soon.
10. My family are visiting Japan next year.
11. Our class won the chess competition this year.
12. Dad met Uncle Ben at the bank this afternoon.

Did You Know

Some **adverbs** tell you **when** the actions happen. They are called **adverbs of time**. They describe verbs and answer the question 'When?'.

 ISBN 978-81-8477-748-2

E Read the poem and answer the questions below.

Ants Everywhere

Tiny ants run everywhere,
Outside, inside, anywhere,
They run up here and run
down there,
Upstairs and downstairs
and everywhere.

Did You Know?

Some **adverbs** tell **where** the actions happen. They are called **adverbs of place**. They give more information about verbs and answer the question 'Where?'

1. What is the verb used in the poem? ____________________
2. List the words in the poem that describe where tiny ants run about:

(a) everywhere ____________ (e) ____________

(b) ____________ (f) ____________

(c) ____________ (g) ____________

(d) ____________ (h) ____________

All these words are adverbs of ____________.

F *Put a circle around the verb in each sentence and ask the question 'Where?'. Then underline the **adverb of place** which answers that question.*

1. Someone is hiding inside.
2. Stay here with the dog.
3. Don't loiter anywhere.
4. Let's go somewhere for a holiday this weekend.
5. This year our school concert will be held outdoors.
6. We will arrive there in the afternoon.

 ISBN 978-81-8477-748-2

G

*Choose a suitable **adverbial** from the two lists in the box to complete each of the sentences.*

Adverbials of place	Adverbials of time
on the top shelf	at 7:00 pm
round the huge castle	from March to June
in the park	in the afternoon

1. The show starts ______________________
2. It usually rains ______________________
3. The tourists walked ______________________
4. I arranged all the books neatly ______________________
5. Sometimes Grandma takes a nap ______________________
6. Alice and her friends often cycle ______________________

Did You Know

An **adverbial** is a group of words that has the same use as an **adverb**. An **adverbial of place** tells **where** an action happens. An **adverbial of time** tells **when** an action happens.

All these adverbials begin with **prepositions** like **in**, **on**, **at**, **round**. These adverbials are also called **prepositional phrases** or **adverbial phrases**.

H

*Underline the **adverbials** in the following sentences. Do they tell you **time** or **place**? Put a tick in the correct box. The first one is done for you.*

		when	where
1.	The boys are playing <u>in the field</u>.	☐	✓
2.	Mary is going to the post office this morning.	☐	☐
3.	The school bus left at eight o'clock.	☐	☐
4.	He is diving into the pool.	☐	☐
5.	There was a big celebration on New Year's Eve.	☐	☐
6.	The joggers are running along the road.	☐	☐
7.	We always have lunch at noon.	☐	☐
8.	The scouts are sitting round the fire.	☐	☐
9.	I will come as soon as possible.	☐	☐
10.	There are lots of cracks in the wall.	☐	☐

 ISBN 978-81-8477-748-2

12 More Adverbs and Adverbials

A *Choose a suitable adverb that answers the question 'How often?' from the box to complete each of the sentences. You may use some adverbs in more than one sentence.*

never	seldom	sometimes	always

1. It ______________ snows in Singapore.
2. I ______________ go horse riding.
3. In the desert it ______________ rains.
4. The sun ______________ rises in the east.
5. I ______________ do my homework without being reminded to do it.

Did You Know?

Some words tell you **how often** someone does something or **how often** something happens. The words are called **adverbs of frequency**.

B *Read the following letter and underline all the adverbs that tell 'How often?'.*

Dear Grandma,

Thank you for your letter. I know I usually write to you at the end of the month, but I'm excited and I can't wait to tell you about something.

Yesterday I asked Mum if I could go ice-skating with my friend Mark on Saturday. I have only done that once before. I have asked her before but she has always refused to let me go. She thinks I could get hurt. I told her that Mark often goes skating and he never gets hurt. Mum seldom lets me go anywhere without her, but this time she said I could go! She also said that if I really like it, I could go sometimes during the holidays.

I can't wait for Saturday to come. I'll write and tell you about it.

Love,
Richard

 ISBN 978-81-8477-748-2

C ***Underline the adverbials in the passage that answer the question 'How often?' Can you find 11 such adverbials? The first one is done for you.***

Did You Know

An **adverbial** is a group of words that has the same use as an **adverb**.

So an **adverbial of frequency** is a group of words that tells you **how often** somebody does something, or **how often** an action happens.

Poor old Mr Potts. He was very bored. Every day, every week and every month seemed the same to him. He lived in a small village and had been out of the village only a few times since he was born.

Twice a year, his sister came to visit him. She seldom stayed longer than a night or two because she needed to visit an orphanage once a week to help look after the children there.

Many times, Mr Potts had tried to find an unusual hobby but every time he started one, he lost interest in it after just a few days. "What hobby can I take up? I need something that I can do three or four times a week."

D ***Choose a suitable adverb that answers the question 'How long?' from the box to fill in each blank in the following text.***

long **longer** **forever** **overnight**

Did You Know

Some words tell you how long someone does something or how long something happens. They are called **adverbs of duration**.

Christmas is really exciting. When you are waiting for something exciting — like Christmas Day — it seems to take __________. Grandma and Grandpa sleep __________ at our place, so they can open presents with us on Christmas Day. I get up very early on Christmas Day, but my grandparents like to sleep __________. I usually do not like to stay in bed __________.

 ISBN 978-81-8477-748-2

E *Choose suitable adverbials from those in the brackets to say how long the action or activity is likely to last. Circle the selected adverbial.*

1. Can you hop (**for five minutes / for a week / for a year**)?
2. We left the peas (**all night / all week / all year**) to germinate.
3. Bears sleep (**through the night / through the year / through the winter**).
4. Summer lasts (**for ever and ever / for a few months / for a short while**).
5. They continued chatting on the phone (**for another hour / for another week / for another fortnight**).

Did You Know

An **adverbial of duration** is a group of words that tells you for **how long** somebody does something, or for **how long** something happens or lasts.

F *Look at the adverbs or adverbials in bold print in the following sentences. Circle the verbs that they are connected with. Then put a tick (✓) in the correct box to show whether the adverbs or adverbials answer the question 'How often?' or 'How long?'.*

	How often?	How long?
1. Miss Lee taught us English **for a term.**	☐	☐
2. Take this cough mixture **three times a day.**	☐	☐
3. Uncle Ben goes to the library **every week.**	☐	☐
4. The dog **always** barks at strangers.	☐	☐
5. It would be good to take a holiday **once in a while.**	☐	☐
6. She stopped **for a moment**, then walked away slowly.	☐	☐
7. It **usually** rains in the afternoon.	☐	☐
8. Dad goes to Europe **a few times a year** for business.	☐	☐
9. The job of painting the big house went on for **two weeks.**	☐	☐
10. She has been talking on the phone **all morning.**	☐	☐
11. You have to practise **for a long time** to be a good musician.	☐	☐
12. The timidest children **hardly ever** say anything.	☐	☐

 ISBN 978-81-8477-748-2

G *Underline the **adverbs or adverbials** in the following sentences. Do they tell you 'how long' or 'how often'? Put a tick in the correct box.*

	how long?	how often?
1. The magazine is published <u>once a month</u>.	☐	✓
2. The school will close for a week.	☐	☐
3. Nobody will live forever.	☐	☐
4. We meet twice a week.	☐	☐
5. I have not seen John for months.	☐	☐
6. Dad takes our dog for a walk every morning.	☐	☐
7. The bus leaves the zoo every hour.	☐	☐
8. The teacher has told him many times not to be late.	☐	☐
9. We have waited for Jeff for an hour.	☐	☐
10. The children go to school every day.	☐	☐
11. The refugees waited for days before help came.	☐	☐
12. I can finish reading a large book in a day.	☐	☐

H *Complete the sentences by adding **adverbials** that tell you 'how often' or 'how long'.*

1. I brush my teeth ________________________________.
2. Sue goes to the library ________________________________.
3. We have maths lessons ________________________________.
4. They went to Hong Kong ________________________________.
5. Our school holidays last ________________________________.
6. I talk to my best friend ________________________________.

 ISBN 978-81-8477-748-2

13 Tenses: The Simple Present and Present Continuous

A *Here is a text written in the present tense. Underline the **present tense action verbs**.*

Did You Know

A verb in the **present tense** describes an action that is done as a habit, or an action that happens regularly.

You also use the present tense when you talk about facts.

In every year there are four seasons — summer, autumn, winter and spring. Each season is about three months long. The weather changes in every season.

Summer is the warmest season with long days. People spend a lot of time outside the house in summer.

Autumn is the time when many trees begin to lose their leaves while they get ready for the cold winter weather.

Winter is the coldest and wettest season of the year. The days are very short and the nights very long.

In spring the weather slowly becomes warmer. The signs of spring are the green shoots and leaves on plants and the sounds of birds and insects.

After spring we return to summer and the cycle begins all over again.

B *Complete the sentences with a suitable verb in the present tense from the box.*

whisper	howls	snarls	rustle	mutters	screams

1. On stormy nights the wind ________________ through the trees.
2. The fierce watchdog often ________________ at trespassers.
3. People usually ________________ when they tell a secret.
4. Grandad sometimes ________________ to himself in a low voice.
5. My sister ________________ every time she sees a cockroach or a frog.
6. The leaves ____________ in the wind and fall to the ground.

 ISBN 978-81-8477-748-2

C *The following part of a report tells you what frogs do. Underline the* ***present tense action verbs.***

Did You Know

You always use **present tense verbs** to write reports on animals and plants, unless they are extinct.

Frogs are animals that live in water and on land. They use their strong back legs to swim and hop. If an enemy approaches, they can bound away quickly. In the daytime in summer, frogs perch on lily pads and sleep, but at night time, they croak loudly to attract a mate.

The female frog lays eggs in still water. These eggs then hatch into tadpoles. Tadpoles, like fish, live in water, so they need to breathe through gills. Later the tadpoles will grow lungs to help them breathe. Gradually the tadpoles develop legs and lose their tails.

D *Write two sentences about things that each of the following animals do. Underline the* ***present tense*** *action verbs you have used.*

1. **Polar bears**

   (a) Polar bears <u>live</u> in cold countries where there is ice and snow.

   (b) ______________________________

2. **Lions**

   (a) ______________________________

   (b) ______________________________

3. **Sharks**

   (a) ______________________________

   (b) ______________________________

 ISBN 978-81-8477-748-2

E *Look at the information in this table and write sentences about what each child likes and doesn't like. Make sure you use the* ***present tense.***

Name	English	likes drama	plays badminton
Catherine	good	Yes	Yes
George	quite good	Yes	No
Paul	weak	No	No
John	good	Yes	No
May	weak	Yes	Yes
Rudy	quite good	No	No
Sue	quite good	No	Yes
Kim	weak	No	Yes

Did You Know

When you state a fact or say something you know about a person or thing, you use the **simple present tense.**

1. Catherine is good at English. She likes drama and plays badminton.
2. George ____________________
3. Paul ____________________
4. John ____________________
5. May ____________________
6. Rudy ____________________
7. Sue ____________________
8. Kim ____________________

 ISBN 978-81-8477-748-2

F *The picture shows the Green family working in the garden. Use the* ***present continuous tense*** *to write about what each member is doing and underline the verbs. Put as much information as you can in each sentence. Use the first one to help you write your own sentences.*

Did You Know ?

You use the **present continuous tense** to talk about actions that are going on or are taking place at the time of speaking.

You form the present continuous tense by adding **am, is** or **are** to a verb ending in **-ing**.

1. Mr and Mrs Green and their children, Joe and Amy, are working in their garden.
2. ____________________
3. ____________________
4. ____________________
5. ____________________

 ISBN 978-81-8477-748-2

G *Use the **present continuous tense** to complete three sentences about each picture.*

The boy is reading a book.

The girl ____________________

____

The dog ____________________

____

The ladies ____________________

____

The juggler ____________________

____

The man ____________________

____

The child ____________________

____

____

____

____

____

The girl ____________________

____

____

____

____

____

 ISBN 978-81-8477-748-2

14 Tenses: The Simple Past and Past Continuous

A *Read the following story. Replace the **past tense verbs** in bold print with a suitable one from the box. Cross out the verb in bold and write the new verb above it.*

realized	scowled	suggested	knocked
returned	dashed	purchased	
adored	left	thought	

Did You Know

You use the **past tense** to talk about actions that happened in the past.

Janet's father **looked** at the broken vase. She **pushed** the vase off the shelf when she **ran** clumsily into the house. Her mother would be very upset because she **liked** that vase. Janet wished she had been more careful but **knew** there was no point regretting. She told her father that she would buy

a similar vase with her pocket money. Her father **said** that if she **bought** it before her mother **got** home, she would not know it was ever broken. Janet **felt** that was a good idea. So they **went** immediately to buy the vase.

 ISBN 978-81-8477-748-2

B *The words in the box are verbs in the past tense form. Group them under the suitable headings in the table.*

knocked	nodded	pushed	worried
raced	tapped	returned	adored
pinned	hurried	closed	cried

Did You Know

You can form the **past tense** in a few ways:

- by adding **-d** to the verb;
- by adding **-ed** to the verb;
- by doubling the last letter of the verb before adding **-ed**;
- by changing the **y** to **i** for verbs ending in **-y** before adding **-ed**.

verb + *-d*	verb + *-ed*	double last letter of verb + *-ed*	change *-y* to *-i* and add *-ed*

C *Circle the correct **past tense verb** for each of the following sentences.*

Did You Know

You do not add **-d** or **-ed** to some verbs, but you change them to a different form for their simple past tense form.

However, there are some verbs which you don't change at all to form the past tense.

1. Uncle Ben (**cutted / cut**) the grass last weekend.
2. We (**carryed / carried**) our luggage to the car.
3. He (**letted / let**) us play outside.
4. Dad (**teached / taught**) me how to whistle.
5. His fans (**was / were**) at the airport to welcome the pop star.
6. Paul accidentally (**hit / hitted**) the window with the ball.
7. The jug (**falled / fell**) off the table and (**broke / breaked**).
8. The bell (**rang / rung**) very loudly at the start of the lesson.
9. Susan (**hurt / hurted**) her leg during the running practice.
10. The villagers (**sang / sing**) and (**danced / dance**) around the fire.

 ISBN 978-81-8477-748-2

D *The words in the box are past tense verbs. You can use them to talk about the ways people move. Sort them under the suitable headings in the table.*

skipped	hurried	crawled	bounced
leaped	raced	danced	strolled
rushed	limped	dashed	staggered

Slow ways to move	Fast ways to move	Happy ways to move

E *Which of the verbs from the table above is suitable for each of the following sentences? Choose one to complete each sentence. In some cases more than one of the verbs may be suitable.*

1. The baby ________________ across the floor to her mother.
2. The injured player ________________ off the football field.
3. Jane ________________ home to tell her parents about the exciting news.
4. The businessman ________________ to catch the train.
5. The girls formed a circle and ________________ round the fire.
6. Mike ________________ into the air for joy when he found out he had been chosen to play in the match.
7. The children ________________ on the trampoline in the gymnasium.
8. Even though he was late, Tim ________________ in very calmly.

 ISBN 978-81-8477-748-2

F *Read the story below and underline the verbs in the* ***past continuous tense.***

Last week our family went to the Spring Festival celebrations. When we arrived, everyone was crowding around to see the parade. Some students were dancing to the music of the band and small children were clapping their hands in delight. Vendors were walking up and down yelling. They were trying to sell their drinks and ice creams. People were singing and dancing in the street. Even the police officers were laughing and joking with the spectators. Only one small boy was crying. I think he was lost.

Did You Know

For actions that were going on some time in the past, or an action that was going on when another one took place, you use the **past continuous tense.**

You form the past continuous tense by adding **was** or **were** to a verb ending in **-ing**.

G *Here is a poem written in the* ***present continuous tense.*** *Rewrite it in the box, using the* ***past continuous tense.***

Exercises at School

We are twisting,
We are turning
And our muscles are burning.

We are jumping,
We are bumping
And our hearts are thumping.

I am stretching,
I am rolling
Because I am bowling.

I am swaying,
I am playing
But my teacher is saying,

"MORE EFFORT, PLEASE!"

Exercises at School

We were twisting, ______________________

____

____

 ISBN 978-81-8477-748-2

15 The Future Tense

A *Use the **simple future tense** to predict something each of the following people will do.*

Did You Know

You form the future tense by using **shall** or **will** with a verb.

You can use **shall** or **will** with **I**.

You use **will** with **you**, **he**, **she**, **it**, **we** and **they**.

1. something you will do this evening
   I ______________________________
   ____
2. something your dad will do tomorrow
   He ______________________________
3. something your sister will do next Saturday
   She ______________________________
4. something your friends Jim and Kumar will do during the school holidays
   They ______________________________
5. something your family will do next New Year holiday
   We ______________________________

B ***What do you think your life as an adult will be like? Answer the following questions using the simple future tense.***

1. Where will you live? ______________________________
   ____
2. What will your occupation be? ______________________________
   ____
3. What will you do in your spare time? ______________________________
   ____
4. Will you learn to drive? ______________________________
   ____

 ISBN 978-81-8477-748-2

C *Write down something you could promise to make the following people happy, using the **future tense**. The first one is done for you as an example.*

Did You Know?

You use the **simple future tense** when you make a promise to do something.

1. Your mother: I promise I will clean up my bedroom this afternoon.
2. Your father: ____________________
3. Your teacher: ____________________
4. Your best friend: ____________________
5. Your brother, sister or cousin: ____________________

D *The children in the pictures are thinking about what they are going to do on the weekend. Write sentences to show what each of them **is going to** do.*

Did You Know?

To talk about things you have planned to do in the future, you can use:

am/is/are + going to + verb

1. Kamal is going ____________________
2. Kim ____________________
3. Mike ____________________

 ISBN 978-81-8477-748-2

E ***Write what these boys and girls are going to do when they leave school. Use is going to + verb in your sentences. The first one is done for you.***

1. Danny is going to be a doctor treating children.

2. Farah ____________________

3. Gary ____________________

4. Linda ____________________

5. Martin ____________________

6. Shanti ____________________

 ISBN 978-81-8477-748-2

F *Here is a page from Lily's diary. It shows what she will be doing next Saturday. Read the diary and answer the questions.*

9 Saturday	**August 2014**
AM	
9:00	catch express bus to city
9:30	buy two files for project work
10:30	return books to the library
11:30	meet Jane for lunch
PM	
12:30	order flowers for Grandma's birthday
1:00	post a letter
2:00	purchase movie tickets
6:00	call Tom about project work

1. What will Lily do on Saturday at these times?
   - At 9:00 am, ______________________________
   - At 10:30 am, ______________________________
   - At 1:00 pm, ______________________________
   - At 6:00 pm, ______________________________

2. What is Lily going to do on Saturday at these times?
   - At 9:30 am, ______________________________
   - At 11:30 am, ______________________________
   - At 12:30 pm, ______________________________
   - At 2:00 pm, ______________________________

 ISBN 978-81-8477-748-2

16 Using the Correct Verbs

A *There are 11 incorrect verbs in the following conversation. Look for the errors and cross them out. Then write the correct verb in the space provided. The first one has been done for you.*

May: My mother is not very happy with me today. I ~~done~~ some silly things yesterday. did

Joe: What did you do?

May: It begun when I tried to help. I cleaned the kitchen cupboard and throwed away a special box she wanted to save. I should have asked her first.

Joe: That doesn't sound like very much to get upset about.

May: No, it don't, but then I ran to answer the door when the bell rings, and I clumsily tripped over the mat and fall onto the floor.

Joe: How can your mother be upset over that? She should have been worrying about whether you had hurt yourself.

May: Well, I knocked over the table and her favourite vase flied up into the air, fell to the floor and broked. I should have been more careful.

Joe: Yes, you sometimes do things without thinking carefully first.

May: After that, Jane come to my house because we had to finish our project. She give me her paper last week but I couldn't find it. I'll try to be careful in the future. I just hope I can find the paper soon.

 ISBN 978-81-8477-748-2

B ***Fill in the blanks with do or does to complete the sentences. Be sure you choose the one that agrees with the subject.***

1. The principal __________ (**do, does**) not like pupils to be late for school.
2. __________ (**Do, Does**) these colours match?
3. Water and oil __________ (**do, does**) not mix.
4. We __________ (**do, does**) not know why he is always absent.
5. She __________ (**do, does**) not feel cold.
6. He __________ (**do, does**) not seem to be well.
7. Uncle Tom __________ (**do, does**) not like curry.
8. These trousers __________ (**do, does**) not fit me.

Did You Know

You use **do** with **I, we, they, you** and **plural nouns**.

You use **does** with **he, she, it** and **singular nouns**.

are / **do** — we, you, they, plural nouns

is / **does** — he, she, it, singular nouns

am / **do** — I

C ***Fill in the blanks with am, is or are to complete the passage. Be sure the verb agrees with the subject.***

Hello, my name __________ Ali and I __________ ten years old. I have two brothers who __________ younger than me. We __________ very close and do everything together. My youngest brother __________ not a very good swimmer, so I __________ teaching him in our pool. My other brother __________ a much stronger swimmer, so the two of us __________ allowed to go to the pool without our parents. When I __________ older, I __________ going to join a swimming club. My brothers want to join too. I hope we __________ able to win some medals.

Did You Know

You use:

- **am** with **I**
- **is** with **he, she, it** and **singular nouns**
- **are** with **you, we, they** and **plural nouns.**

 ISBN 978-81-8477-748-2

D *Circle the correct verb in brackets in the following sentences.*

1. John and his family (**is / are**) going to Sydney on holiday.
2. Each child (**has / have**) a new book to read on Monday mornings.
3. The new teacher (**talks / talk**) too quickly for me to understand her.
4. Every one of these apples (**is / are**) rotten.

Did You Know

You use **singular verbs** with **singular nouns**.

You use **plural verbs** with **plural nouns**.

You use a **singular verb** with these words: **each**, **either**, **every**, **nobody** and **everybody**.

5. Nobody (**are / is**) allowed to enter the library if the librarian isn't there.
6. James (**was / were**) present but his friends (**was / were**) not.
7. Either Jane or Sue (**is / are**) running in the race.
8. The boys and the girl (**is / are**) helping the teacher with the display.

E *Some verbs in the following sentences are used incorrectly. Rewrite the sentences using the correct verbs.*

1. Our class include several students from other countries.

   ____

2. Neither Susan nor Farah belong to the Red Cross Club.

   ____

3. The player were sent off for rough play.

   ____

4. Everyone at the party were having fun.

   ____

 ISBN 978-81-8477-748-2

17 Modals

A *The following signs show some of the things you **must not** do in the National Park. Write down what the signs say you **must not** do. The first one is done for you.*

1.  no lighting fires	2.  no fishing	3.  no camping
4.  no littering	5.  no feeding monkeys	6.  no picking flowers

1. You must not light a fire in the National Park.
2. ______________________________
3. ______________________________
4. ______________________________
5. ______________________________
6. ______________________________

B *Write down three things you must remember to do when you cross a busy street.*

1. ______________________________
   ____
2. ______________________________
   ____
3. ______________________________
   ____

 ISBN 978-81-8477-748-2

C *Look at the pictures and write down what it is that the person* ***should not*** *be doing. Then write down what they* ***ought to*** *do instead.*

Did You Know

You can use **ought to** and **should** to say something you do as a duty. The words are called **modal verbs.**

1. The girl should not throw rubbish on the ground.
   She ought to put it in the rubbish bin near the tree.

2. Sharon ______

3. Tom ______

4. The boys ______

 ISBN 978-81-8477-748-2

D *Read what happened to John and some of his family members.*
Use ***ought to*** *and* ***should/shouldn't*** *to offer advice to them as in No. 1.*

1. John was playing near a deep pond. He fell in and nearly drowned.

   John ought to be more careful.

   He shouldn't play near deep water if he can't swim.

   He ought to learn to swim.

2. John's father coughs loudly every morning. He smokes a packet of cigarettes every day.

   ____

   ____

   ____

3. May always fails her English exams. She plays video games. She doesn't read much.

   ____

   ____

   ____

4. Tom likes to be first. He pushes other children out of the queue.

   ____

   ____

   ____

5. John's grandmother is very old and needs help every day. A lot of time, John just plays with his friends.

   ____

   ____

   ____

 ISBN 978-81-8477-748-2

E *Look at the pictures and write a sentence about some good habits that a student must have for each picture. You can use* ***should, ought to*** *or* ***must*** *with verbs in your sentences.*

1. A good student must be punctual.

2.

3.

4.

5.

6.

 ISBN 978-81-8477-748-2

18 Sentences

A *Read the following. Put a tick (✓) against those that are sentences, and a cross (✗) against those that are not sentences.*

		Sentence
1.	The whole class went.	
2.	The park is a good place for a picnic.	
3.	The rain came down suddenly.	
4.	Later, we played games.	
5.	Ate our lunch.	
6.	In the park.	
7.	We were cold.	
8.	I saw my friends there.	
9.	At the concert.	
10.	When you are ready.	
11.	We play after school.	
12.	Violets are blue.	

Did You Know?

A **sentence** begins with a capital letter and ends with a full stop, or a question mark, or an exclamation mark.

A **simple sentence** must have a complete meaning. It must have a **subject** and a **verb**. The **subject** refers to the person or thing that does the **action**.

B *Change the non-sentences above to sentences by adding the missing parts. Remember the missing parts may be the subject or the verb.*

1. ______________________________

2. ______________________________

3. ______________________________

4. ______________________________

5. ______________________________

 ISBN 978-81-8477-748-2

C ***Read the sentences below and identify the subject and predicate. Write them in the table below. The first one is done for you.***

1. The dog growled fiercely.
2. Cats like fish.
3. Her hair is black.
4. Birds have feathers.
5. The baby is sleeping in the cot.
6. Aunt Sarah sent me a postcard.
7. Jenny's mother scolded her.
8. Everyone knows that!
9. None of us heard the telephone ringing.
10. She wrote a poem about the cat.

Did You Know

A sentence has two main parts: the **subject** and the **predicate**.

The **subject** refers to the person or thing that does the action. The **predicate** refers to the verb together with the rest of the sentence.

Subject	Predicate
1. The dog	growled fiercely
2.	
3.	
4.	
5.	
6.	
7.	
8.	
9.	
10.	

 ISBN 978-81-8477-748-2

D *Read the sentences below and identify the* ***subject, verb and object.*** *Write them correctly in the table below. The first one is done for you.*

1. The dog has a new collar.
2. Mary is sharpening her pencil.
3. This machine makes a lot of noise.
4. They are playing table tennis.
5. He was repairing the telephone.
6. Susan likes singing.
7. A barber cuts hair.
8. The author wrote an animal story.
9. Everyone enjoyed the show.
10. Dad is reading a magazine.

Did You Know

The predicate of a sentence is made up of a **verb** and, sometimes, an **object**. The **object** refers to the person or thing that receives the action done by the **subject**.

Subject	Verb	Object
1. The dog	has	a new collar
2.		
3.		
4.		
5.		
6.		
7.		
8.		
9.		
10.		

 ISBN 978-81-8477-748-2

E *Read the sentences below. Circle the **direct object** and underline the **indirect object**. The first one is done for you.*

1. Dad gave the children a chocolate.
2. Mum is making the baby some milk.
3. Miss Lee allowed the children five minutes to settle down.
4. The young man wrote the girl a letter.
5. She is singing us a song.
6. The policeman showed the tourist the way to the castle.
7. The girl offered the old lady her seat.
8. The instructor taught him driving.
9. The teacher told us the story of early Singapore.
10. Paul gave Peter some stamps.
11. The waitress brought me a glass of milk.
12. Miss Lee gave Tom his report card.
13. She showed her friends her wedding photos.
14. The boy told the policeman what he saw.
15. The manager gave each staff member a gift.

Did You Know

Some verbs have two objects: a **direct object** and an **indirect object**. You can find the **direct object** by asking 'what' after the verb. You can find the **indirect object** by asking 'who' is receiving the direct object.

 ISBN 978-81-8477-748-2

19 More about Sentences

A *Here are some **simple sentences**. Add information to tell more about the word in bold print in each sentence. The first one is done for you.*

1. The boy bought a **robot**. (*Add an adjective.*)

   The boy bought an expensive robot.

2. The **teacher** praised the class. (*Add an adjective.*)

   ____

3. The lion **roared**. (*Add an adverb that tells how.*)

   ____

4. The lady saw a **mouse**. (*Add an adjective.*)

   ____

5. The children **were playing**. (*Add an adverb that tells where.*)

   ____

6. The movie **started**. (*Add an adverbial that tells when.*)

   ____

7. Mrs Lee **walked** to the bus stop. (*Add an adverbial that tells how.*)

   ____

8. They **ate** their picnic lunch. (*Add an adverb that tells how.*)

   ____

9. Mr Kamal bought a **car**. (*Add an adjective.*)

   ____

10. The children **coloured** the pictures. (*Add an adverb that tells how.*)

    ____

Did You Know

A **simple sentence** often has extra words added to give more information. You add **adverbs** or **adverbials** to give more information about verbs and **adjectives** to give more information about nouns.

The sentence will be longer and contain more information, but it will still have only one main idea.

 ISBN 978-81-8477-748-2

B *The words in bold print in the sentences are adjectives. Which noun does the adjective describe in each sentence? Write your answer on the line.*

1. Mr Omar dozes off in his **comfortable** armchair. ____________
2. They are all **talented** musicians. ____________
3. The author talked about his **interesting** life story. ____________
4. The **elegant** lady over there is my aunt. ____________
5. The **early** bird catches the worm. ____________
6. On a **quiet** afternoon, two strangers appeared at our house. ____________
7. The cart moved slowly along the **muddy** track. ____________
8. Suddenly we heard a **loud** roar across the river. ____________

C *The words in bold print in the sentences are adverbs or adverbials. Write the verbs they are connected with on the lines. Then put a tick (✓) in the correct box to say whether the adverbs or adverbials tell you 'how' or 'where' or 'when' the action happens in each sentence.*

Remember

An **adverb** is usually one word, and an **adverbial** is a group of words. Both are used to modify **verbs**.

	Sentence	Verb	how	where	when
1.	The soldiers fought **bravely** in the war.	________	☐	☐	☐
2.	Get **inside** before it starts to rain.	________	☐	☐	☐
3.	Siva came **early** to help us paint the house.	________	☐	☐	☐
4.	I think Mum is resting **upstairs**.	________	☐	☐	☐
5.	The actors bowed **politely** to the audience.	________	☐	☐	☐
6.	The manager wants to see you **now**.	________	☐	☐	☐
7.	Mr Chen drove **down the road**.	________	☐	☐	☐
8.	He wrote the letter **in his best handwriting**.	________	☐	☐	☐
9.	It jumped **over the fence**.	________	☐	☐	☐
10.	The bird sings **in the morning**.	________	☐	☐	☐

 ISBN 978-81-8477-748-2

D ***Read the instructions in the box on the left and find the part that has been added to each group of words or sentence on the right. Underline those words.***

• *Begin with a noun* (a subject).	1. The dragon
• *Add an adjective* (information about the noun).	2. The fiery dragon
• *Add another adjective and a comma.*	3. The fearsome, fiery dragon
• *Add a verb or a verb group* (action done by the subject).	4. The fearsome, fiery dragon soared.
• *Add an adverb that tells 'how'* (information about the verb).	5. The fearsome, fiery dragon soared menacingly.
• *Add an adverb or adverbial that tells 'where'.*	6. The fearsome, fiery dragon soared menacingly over the hills.

E ***Follow the 6 steps in the box above to make a group of words or sentence of your own that begins with 'The man'.***

1. The man ______________________
2. ______________________
3. ______________________
4. ______________________

   ____
5. ______________________

   ____
6. ______________________

   ____

 ISBN 978-81-8477-748-2

F ***Read these groups of sentences and write down what type each sentence is. The first one has been done for you.***

Did You Know

There are 4 types of sentences you can use:

- A **statement** to tell a fact. It ends with a full stop.
- A **question** to ask about something or someone. It ends with a question mark.
- An **imperative** to give orders or instructions. It ends with a full stop or an exclamation mark.
- An **exclamation** to express yourself strongly, sometimes with the verb missing. It ends with an exclamation mark.

1. What a delicious cake! (an exclamation)
2. I made it myself. (__________________)
3. How did you make it? (__________________)
4. Easy! (__________________)
5. Tell me how. (__________________)
6. Mix three cups of flour, two eggs, some chocolate pieces , a cup of milk and a cup of sugar. (__________________)

7. Why are you sitting there? (__________________)
8. Go away! (__________________)
9. I'm watching for birds and you are scaring them away. (__________________)
10. May I help you? (__________________)
11. Please hold these binoculars for me. (__________________)

12. Help! A snake! (__________________)
13. Where? What kind is it? (__________________)
14. It's a cobra and it's very dangerous. (__________________)
15. Don't make a noise. Walk quietly away. (__________________)

 ISBN 978-81-8477-748-2

20 Questions

A *What could the person have asked to get these answers? Write the question for each answer.*

> **Did You Know ?**
>
> A **question** is a sentence which asks something. It always ends with a **question mark**.
>
> You can use any of these helping verbs to ask questions; **am, is, are, was, were, do, have, will, may, can.**

1. ____________________________________

   No, thank you. I'm not hungry.

2. ____________________________________

   Yes, we were in the same class last year.

3. ____________________________________

   No, I don't have a pencil.

4. ____

   You may come with me to the park.

5. ____

   I won't be able to help you do your homework.

6. ____

   Yes, I wanted to go, but I can't now.

7. ____

   Yes, I will be free to help you on Sunday.

8. ____

   I shall be there. I promise!

9. ____

   It's rather cold in here.

10. ____

    I've brushed my teeth and combed my hair.

 ISBN 978-81-8477-748-2

B *Write a yes-answer and a no-answer to each question. The first one is done for you.*

Did You Know

When a question has a **helping verb** and a **main verb**, the **subject** comes between them.

1. Do cats like fish?

   Yes, cats like fish.

   No, cats don't like fish.

2. Do plants grow in the desert?

3. Did you sleep well last night?

4. Does your mother like strawberries?

C *Write a yes-answer and a no-answer to each question. Try to use contractions in your answers. The first one is done for you.*

1. Have you got an atlas?

   Yes, I've got an atlas.

   No, I haven't got an atlas.

2. Has John handed in his homework?

3. Has the postman delivered the mail?

4. Have you read any Harry Potter stories?

 ISBN 978-81-8477-748-2

D *Read the dialogue below and underline the* ***question words.***

A police officer is questioning a person near the scene of a bank robbery.

Officer : What's your name, and what were you doing in this area?

Man : My name is Johnson Lin. I was waiting for my friend.

Officer : Who is your friend? What's his name?

Man : His name is Ramu. We live near each other.

Officer : Where do you live?

Man : I live next to the railway station. My friend lives on the other side of the station.

Officer : When were you supposed to meet this friend of yours, and why were you meeting him?

Man : At 6:00 pm. We were going to the movies.

Officer : Which movie were you going to?

Man : The one being shown at the Lido cinema inside this building.

Officer : How did you get here?

Man : I took a bus and then walked from the bus stop over there.

Officer : There has been a robbery at the bank. Did you see anyone acting suspiciously when you arrived?

Man : No, I didn't see anyone or anything strange.

Office : OK! You're free to go now. But I may need to ask you some more questions later.

 ISBN 978-81-8477-748-2

E Complete the questions with *when, why, where and how.*

1. ____________ don't you say something?
2. ____________ does the rainy season begin?
3. ____________ did the robbers hide the treasure?
4. ____________ did you go to America?
5. ____________ and ____________ was he born?
6. ____________ are they always quarrelling?
7. ____________ don't you take a rest?
8. ____________ do you spell the word encyclopedia?
9. ____________ did he come from?
10. ____________ is his face so red?
11. ____________ did he get in here?
12. ____________ can he be so rude?

Did You Know

You use **where, when, why** and **how** to ask questions. These words are called **interrogative adverbs.** They are sometimes called **wh-words.**

F Write *what, who, whose, whom or which* in the blanks to complete the questions.

1. ____________ was the founder of Singapore?
2. ____________ are you going to do next week?
3. ____________ is the author of Treasure Island?
4. No, this is not my pen. ____________ is it then?
5. ____________ is the matter with you?
6. ____________ is brighter, yellow or blue?
7. ____________ of these dresses is yours?
8. ____________ turned off my computer?
9. ____________ is the weather like today?
10. ____________ is Ali's occupation?
11. ____________ is soap made of?
12. To ____________ is she talking?
13. ____________ are you?
14. ____________ is this cat?
15. ____________ of these is mine?

Did You Know

You can also use the pronouns **what, who, whose, whom, which** to ask questions. They are called **interrogative pronouns.**

 ISBN 978-81-8477-748-2

21 Connectors

A *Use **or**, **but** or **and** to join each pair of sentences. Can you leave any words out in your answer? The first one is done for you.*

1. Janet is good at maths. Janet is good at science.
   Janet is good at maths and science.
2. We tried really hard. We did not win.
3. I might go by train. I might go by bus.
4. She likes the watch. She has no money to buy it.
5. The Prince was tall. The prince was handsome.
6. Do your homework. You will not watch TV tonight.
7. John drew a horse as carefully as he could. It looked like a donkey.
8. The lamp was switched off. Jane was soon asleep.

Did You Know

Connectors are words that join words or sentences. They are also called **conjunctions**.

You use **and** to join two sentences when the second sentence tells about what you expect to happen.

You use **but** to join two sentences when the second sentence tells you something you don't expect to happen.

You use **or** to join two sentences when the second sentence refers to a choice.

 ISBN 978-81-8477-748-2

B Complete the passage with the connectors *or, and* or *but.*

It was the end-of-term holidays __________ the children couldn't decide whether to go swimming __________ to go to the movies. They talked about it for a long time, __________ they couldn't come to a decision. Finally they decided to toss a coin __________ the decision was made. They would go swimming.

The next day the children dressed quickly __________ packed their swimming gear, __________ just as they were walking out of the door it began to rain. "I guess it's off to the movies after all," smiled Mum.

C Complete each of these sentences.

1. The children were excited **because** __________
__________.
2. He was not allowed to go **since** __________
__________.
3. You may go home a bit early today **as** __________
__________.
4. He was very scared **for** he didn't know __________
__________.
5. **Since** they were no longer friends __________
__________.
6. __________
__________ **because** it was too hot.
7. __________
__________ **as** it was his birthday.
8. __________
__________ **for** it was not his fault.

Did You Know

Connectors such as **because, for** and **since** are used to join two sentences when the second sentence tells about a **reason.**

 ISBN 978-81-8477-748-2

D *The sentences in the following text are all jumbled up. Rearrange them correctly. Look for the **connectors of time** to help you.*

Finally, he tidies his desk and puts his dirty clothes in the laundry basket.

Then he washes the breakfast dishes.

His mother gives him a hug when he has finished.

First, he cleans his own room.

Ever since he was a small boy, David has been helping his mother.

Before he goes to school, David helps his mother tidy the apartment.

After he has cleaned his room, he begins sweeping the kitchen.

Did You Know

You use words such as **when, while, before, after, since, first, next** and **then** to join two sentences when the second sentence tells about **time** or **order**. These words are called **connectors of time**.

Ever since he was a small boy,

 ISBN 978-81-8477-748-2

E ***Read the following facts about echidnas. Add a suitable connector from the box to complete each sentence.***

first	because	but	and	so that
then	although	when	since	after

1. Echidnas are egg-laying mammals. They are commonly called anteaters ________________ they eat termites and ants. They use their snouts to dig in the sand to uncover the ants, ________________ they use their claws to tear apart rotting timber to find termites.

2. ________________ echidnas are covered with stout spines and bristly hair, their enemies won't want to eat them.

3. ________________ echidnas are small animals, about the size of a cat, they are very strong.

4. Echidnas usually live alone, ________________ they will live together ________________ there is a shortage of shelter.

5. During breeding season, the female echidna prepares a nursery burrow. ______________ she digs a hole about one metre long. ______________ she fills it with grass and leaves. ________________ that she lays her eggs and covers the burrow entrance with dirt ________________ other animals can't find the eggs.

 ISBN 978-81-8477-748-2

22 Punctuation

A *The following are pairs of sentences. Write out the two sentences of each pair, using full stops and capital letters.*

1. wading birds have long legs ducks have short legs

2. helen wants to be a teacher her mother is a lawyer

3. chinatown has lots of chinese restaurants there are also lots of western restaurants there

4. dr smith works in the national eye hospital he drives to work every morning

5. in countries like china and japan, winter starts from december and ends in february in australia, the seasons are opposite to those in china and japan

Did You Know

Full stops are used to show the end of a statement. The next statement then begins with a **capital letter**.

B *Put a full stop at the end of the statements and a question mark at the end of the questions.*

1. Could you say that again
2. They are having a tennis lesson
3. Where do you live
4. Who knows the answer
5. Can you solve this problem for me
6. How many brothers do you have
7. I will wash the dishes after the meal
8. He asked them where they lived

 ISBN 978-81-8477-748-2

C ***Write possible questions for these answers. Don't forget to put a question mark at the end of your questions.***

1. My grandmother is eighty-two years old.

   ____

2. I think it opens at 7:00 am.

   ____

3. John's gone to the movies.

   ____

4. I like books about dinosaurs.

   ____

5. My favourite sport is badminton.

   ____

6. My best friend is Rachel.

   ____

D ***Look at the pictures. Complete the sentences by writing a list of things you can see in each picture. Remember to use commas to separate the items in your sentences.***

> **Did You Know?**
> You use **commas** to separate a list of items in a sentence.

1. 

   In my school bag, I have ______________________________

   ____

   ____

2. On the mat, I can see ______________________________

   ____

   ____

3. 

   In the playground, there are ______________________________

   ____

   ____

 ISBN 978-81-8477-748-2

E ***Rewrite the sentences below, putting capital letters, commas, full stops or question marks in the correct places.***

1. the sun has nine planets they are mercury venus earth mars jupiter saturn uranus neptune and pluto mercury is the smallest planet and jupiter is the largest

2. a long time ago there was a greek storyteller whose name was aesop he told lots of stories called fables fables are stories with a moral a moral is a piece of good advice about how to behave

3. my brother and I went to mark's birthday party on saturday everyone had a good time mark had eight candles on his cake and everyone sang the happy birthday song when he blew them out

 ISBN 978-81-8477-748-2

Page 4
A Teacher check.

Page 5
B Homes: an, a, an, a, a
Pets: a, an, a, a, an, a, an, a

Page 6
C 1. a, the 2. the, the
3. an, the 4. The, an, the
5. An, The 6. the, the, a
D 0, the, the, the, 0, 0, 0, a, an, a, 0, 0, a, the, the, the, the, a

Page 7
E a, the, the, a, the, a, the, the, the, The, the, the, the, the, the, the, the, the

Page 8
A

People	Places
1. clown	1. park
2. astronaut	2. gym
3. acrobat	3. theatre
4. twins	4. field

Animals	Things
1. dolphin	1. robot
2. amphibian	2. scarecrow
3. dinosaur	3. book
4. monkey	4. apron

Page 9
B *Underlined nouns*:
1. grandad, present 2. woman, book
3. man, lawn 4. chairs, desks
5. farmers, crops 6. people, station
7. chests, cave 8. children, computer
9. stepmother, stepdaughter
10. workmen, building
11. rain, month 12. king, queen, palace
13. walk, beach 14. rooster
15. lioness, prey

Page 10
C

Uncountable Noun	Countable Noun	Plural
snow	island	islands
tea	sandwich	sandwiches
work	valley	valley
plastic	shape	shapes
toast	spaceman	spacemen
milk	diary	diaries
dust	echo	echoes
furniture	scarf	scarfs, scarves
bread	mouse	mice
air	half	halves

Page 11
D

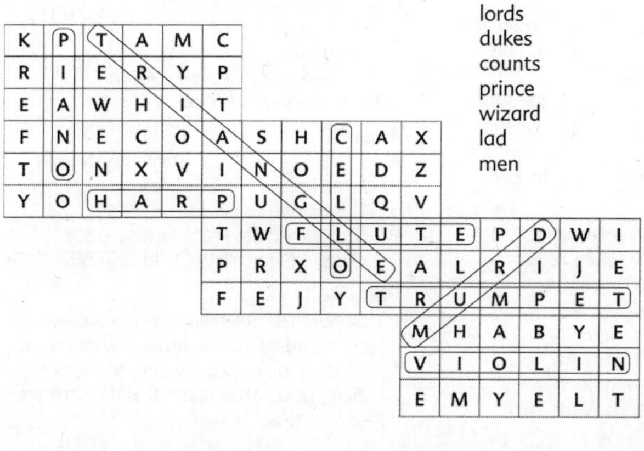

	Plural
1. triangle	triangles
2. violin	violins
3. cello	cellos
4. flute	flutes
5. trumpet	trumpets
6. harp	harp
7. piano	pianos
8. drum	drums

Page 12
A Answers may vary.
B 1. The Adventures of Tom Sawyer
2. The Wolf and the Seven Little Kids
3. The Golden Goose
4. Harry Potter and the Chamber of Secrets
5. Little Red Riding Hood
6. Home Alone
7. Jurassic Park
8. My First Science Dictionary

Page 13
C 1. The guests stayed in the Royal Hotel in Green St.
2. We are going to climb Mount Faber tomorrow.
3. Janet is reading the story of Peter Pan.
4. Lots of visitors like to go to Orchard Road for shopping.
5. Those students go to Thames Public School in London.
6. Christmas falls on 25th of December.
7. The explorers reached the South Pole in June.
8. The Brazilians are very good football players.
9. My mother bought some French perfume in Paris.
10. Dad said John could go to the Star Cinema on Wednesday with David.

Page 14
D Answers may vary.

Page 15
E Answers may vary.

Page 16
A queen, king, females, ladies, duchesses, countesses, prince, witch, girl (lass), women

Masculine Nouns	Feminine Nouns
king	queen
males	females
lords	ladies
dukes	duchesses
counts	countesses
prince	princess
wizard	witch
lad	girl (lass)
men	women

The common-gender noun is guests.

Page 17
B

Feminine	Masculine	Common-gender
leopardess	buck	cattle
vixen	ram	mouse
mare	drake	pupil
housemaid	landlord	engineer
niece	butler	cousin
matron	monk	president

C Teacher check.

Page 18
D 1. an audience 2. a choir
3. a crew 4. a committee
5. an orchestra 6. a family
7. a class 8. a team

Page 19
E 1. ships 2. kittens/puppies/cubs
3. flowers 4. lions
5. cattle/buffaloes/elephants
6. bees 7. steps/stairs/swans
8. flowers/keys/grapes
9. bananas 10. fish/herring
F 2. a string 3. a clump 4. a block
5. an army 6. a flock 7. a pack
8. a litter

Page 20
A 1. It 2. He 3. They 4. They
5. It 6. We 7. her 8. him
9. her 10. them

Page 21
B 1. She 2. We 3. it
4. they 5. you 6. He
C 1. you 2. her 3. us 4. it
5. me 6. them 7. me 8. him

Page 22
D **Holiday Plans**
She, them, they, she, He, I, we, They, me, they, it, me, I, us, we, you, I, I

Page 23
E 2. the Eiffel Tower
3. an Indian emperor; the Taj Mahal
4. Dad and I 5. Your shoes
6. Granny 7. Paul and Peter
8. Alice 9. the tortoise
10. the wind 11. Peter
12. Johnson, Sue and I
13. computers 14. computer

Page 24–25
A 2. These are bicycles and those are tricycles.
3. This is a puppy and that is a dog.
4. This is a python and that is a tiger.
5. This is a caterpillar and that is a butterfly.

Page 26
B 1. ourselves 2. herself
3. themselves 4. myself
5. yourself 6. himself
7. yourselves 8. ourselves
9. herself 10. itself
11. ourselves 12. itself
13. himself 14. ourselves
15. yourself

Page 27
C *Underlined pronouns*: yours, mine, yours, mine, mine, yours, mine, ours, theirs, theirs. ours, Hers, yours, Mine
Circled adjectives: their, your, my, your,

 ISBN 978-81-8477-748-2

our, my

D 2. mine 3. hers 4. his
5. yours 6. theirs 7. ours

Page 28

E 2. Curtis's pony
3. The twins' rabbits
4. Mr Jones's monkey
5. Kelvin's parrots
6. The boys' white rats

F 1. Jill's 2. Joe's
3. Miss Lee's 4. Uncle Jim's
5. Peter's

Page 29

A *Underlined adjectives*:
tired, nervous, sad, excited, eager, frightened, happy, contented, glad, departing, inward-bound, customs, tropical

Page 30

B 1. huge 2. injured
3. strange 4. torn
5. difficult 6. pleasant
7. sharp 8. rare
9. hostile 10. distant

C 2. dusty 3. national
4. homely 5. childish
6. dangerous 7. loving/lovely
8. graceful/gracious 9. musical
10. juicy 11. foolish
12. comfortable

Page 31

D 1. living 2. working
3. crowded 4. frightening
5. barking 6. describing
7. bearded 8. gifted
9. broken 10. stolen
11. used 12. interesting

Page 32

E 1. happy; birthday 2. difficult; language
3. thick; book 4. loud; explosion
5. beautiful; garden 6. colourful; dresses
7. correct; answers 8. special; gift

F Answers may vary.

Page 33

A heavier, taller, less athletic, biggest, stupidest/least clever, least, slower, faster, worst, less, saddest

B

	Comparative	Superlative
2.	more graceful	most graceful
3.	more delicious	most delicious
4.	narrower	narrowest
5.	more dangerous	most dangerous
6.	naughtier	naughtiest
7.	more attractive	most attractive
8.	funnier	funniest

Page 34

C 1. faster 2. prettiest
3. coldest 4. biggest
5. sunnier 6. best
7. stronger 8. younger

D 1. black 2. white
3. red 4. blue
5. brown 6. green
7. pink 8. yellow

Page 35

E 1. oldest 2. youngest
3. tallest 4. old
5. shorter 6. heaviest
7. taller 8. lighter

9. older, younger 10. lighter, heavier

Page 36

F slow—snail timid—mouse
cunning—fox strong—ox
big—whale slippery—eel
brave—lion stubborn—mule

G Answers may vary.

Page 37

A *Underlined determiners*: some, some, some, some, lots of, plenty, several, much, many, each, much, much, all, each, lots of, a few

B 1. much 2. many 3. much
4. much 5. many 6. many

Page 38

C 1. any 2. some 3. any
4. any 5. some 6. some
7. any 8. Some

D 2. Yes, there are some.
No, there aren't any shirts with stripes.
3. Yes, there are some.
No, there aren't any girls in the queue.
4. Yes, there are some.
No, there aren't any cakes on the plate.

Page 39

E 1. a few 2. A few 3. a little
4. a few 5. a few 6. a little
7. a few 8. a little 9. a few
10. a little 11. a few 12. a little
13. a few 14. a few 15. a little

Page 40

F A Damper of a Day
a few, Several, all, all, Several/a few, a few, all, a few/several, several, a few

Page 41

A *Underlined prepositions*: from, in, under, Beside, into, over, in
Circled prepositions: at, until, As, before, at, on

Page 42

B 2. from; time 3. by; time
4. near, to; place 5. until; time
6. off; place 7. beside; place
8. along, across; place
9. through; place 10. up; place

Page 43

C 1. with 2. by 3. of
4. on, on 5. with 6. of
7. for 8. with, for 9. by, for
10. with

D to, on, at, at, by

Page 44

E 1. of 2. near, in 3. down, for
4. from, in 5. for 6. off, on
7. with, to 8. of/about

F 1. besides—beside 2. for—of
3. in—on 4. by—in
5. from—to 6. on—in
7. in—at 8. by—on

Page 45

A 1. quietly 2. correctly
3. angrily 4. cheerfully
5. enormously 6. nicely
7. untidily 8. politely
9. rudely 10. happily

B 1. adjective 2. adverb
3. adverb 4. adjective
5. adverb 6. adverb
7. adjective 8. adjective

Page 46

C 2. disappeared—mysteriously
3. spoke—calmly
4. shouted—angrily
5. studied—hard
6. walked—slowly
7. divided—equally
8. shone—brightly
9. is sleeping—soundly
10. dried—quickly
11. danced—gracefully
12. packed—hastily
13. welcomed—warmly
14. waited—patiently
15. waved—cheerfully

Page 47

D 1. finish—today
2. visited—yesterday
3. will start—tomorrow
4. handed in—late
5. arrived—early
6. leave—now
7. were—last year
8. I'll talk—later
9. leaving—soon
10. are visiting—next year
11. won—this year
12. met—this afternoon

Page 48

E 1. run
2. (b) outside (c) inside
(d) anywhere (e) here
(f) there (g) upstairs
(h) downstairs
All these words are adverbs of place.

F 1. is hiding—inside
2. Stay—here
3. Don't loiter—anywhere
4. go—somewhere
5. will be held—outdoors
6. arrive—there

Page 49

G 1. at 7:00 pm
2. from March to June
3. round the huge castle
4. on the top shelf
5. in the afternoon
6. in the park

H 2. this morning—when
3. at eight o'clock—when
4. into the pool—where
5. on New Year's Eve—when
6. along the road—where
7. at noon—when
8. round the fire—where
9. as soon as possible—when
10. in the wall—where

Page 50

A 1. never 2. Answer may vary.
3. never 4. always
5. Answer may vary.

B *Underlined adverbs*: usually, once, always, often, never, seldom, sometimes

Page 51

C *Underlined adverbials*: every week, every month, a few times, Twice a year, only seldom, once a week, Many times, every time, after just a few days, three or four times a week

 ISBN 978-81-8477-748-2

D forever, overnight, longer, long

Page 52

E 1. for five minutes
2. all night
3. through the winter
4. for a few months
5. for another hour

F 1. taught—how long 2. Take—how often
3. goes—how often 4. barks—how often
5. take—how often 6. stopped—how long
7. rains—how often 8. goes—how often
9. went on—how long
10. has been talking—how long
11. have to practise—how long
12. say—how often

Page 53

G 2. for a week—how long
3. forever—how long
4. twice a week—how often
5. for months—how long
6. every morning—how often
7. every hour—how often
8. many times—how often
9. for an hour—how long
10. every day—how often
11. for days —how long
12. in a day—how long

H Answers may vary.

Page 54

A *Underlined words*: changes, spend, begin, get, becomes, return, begins

B 1. howls 2. snarls 3. whisper
4. mutters 5. screams 6. rustle

Page 55

C *Underlined words:* live, use, approaches, can bound, perch, sleep, croak, lays, hatch, live, need, develop, lose

D Answers may vary.

Page 56

E *Suggested answers*:
2. George is quite good at English. He likes drama, but he doesn't play badminton.
3. Paul is weak at English. He doesn't like drama and he doesn't play badminton.
4. John likes drama, but he doesn't play badminton. He is good at English.
5. May likes drama, but is weak at English. She plays badminton.
6. Rudy doesn't like drama and he doesn't play badminton. He's quite good at English.
7. Sue is quite good at English, but she doesn't like drama. She plays badminton.
8. Kim is weak at English and she doesn't like drama. She plays badminton.

Page 57

F *Suggested answers*:
2. Mrs Green is planting seedlings in the garden.
3. Mr Green is raking leaves on the lawn.
4. Amy is sweeping leaves on the path.
5. Joe is watering the plants.

Page 58

G *Suggested answers:*
The girl is making a sandcastle.
The dog is digging a hole in the sand.
The ladies are riding a horse.
The juggler is throwing pins in the air.
The man is swinging on the trapeze.

The child is crying.
The boy is eating an ice cream.
The policeman is helping the old lady cross the road.

The girl is skipping.
One boy is playing basketball.
The other two boys are eating lunch.

Page 59

A scowled, knocked, dashed, adored, realized, suggested, puschased, returned, thought, left

Page 60

B

v + -d	v + -ed	double last letter + -ed	change -y to -i + -ed
raced	knocked	nodded	worried
closed	pushed	pinned	cried
adored	returned	tapped	hurried

C 1. cut 2. carried 3. let
4. taught 5. were 6. hit
7. fell, broke 8. rang 9. hurt
10. sang, danced

Page 61

D *Slow ways*: limped, crawled, strolled, staggered
Fast ways: rushed, hurried, raced, dashed
Happy ways: skipped, leaped, danced, bounced

E 1. crawled 2. limped/staggered
3. any in 2nd column could be accepted
4. any in 2nd column could be accepted
5. danced 6. leaped
7. bounced 8. strolled

Page 62

F *Underlined verbs*:
was crowding, were dancing, were clapping, were walking, were trying, were singing and dancing, were laughing and joking, was crying

G We were twisting,
We were turning
And our muscles were burning.
We were jumping,
We were bumping
And our hearts were thumping.
I was stretching,
I was rolling
Because I was bowling.
I was swaying,
I was playing
But my teacher was saying,
"MORE EFFORT PLEASE!"

Page 63

A Answers may vary.
B Answers may vary.

Page 64

C Answers may vary.

D 1. Kamal is going to play badminton on the weekend.
2. Kim is going to a movie on the weekend.
3. Mike is going to read a book on the weekend.

Page 65

E *Suggested answers*:
1. Danny is going to be a teacher/ work in a kindergarten.
2. Farah is going to be a nurse/doctor/ pharmacist/radiographer.
3. Gary is going to be a fireman.
4. Linda is going to be a cook/waitress.
5. Martin is going to be a manager/ typist/clerk.
6. Shanti is going to be a police officer/ detective.

Page 66

F *Suggested answers*:
1. At 9:00 am, Lily will catch an express bus to the city.
At 10:30 am, she will go to the library to return some books.
At 1:00 pm, she will go to the post office to post a letter.
At 6:00 pm, she will call Tom to talk about a project work.
2. At 9:30 am, Lily is going to buy two files for her project work.
At 11:30 am, she is going to meet Jane for lunch.
At 12:30 pm, she is going to order flowers for Grandma's birthday.
At 2:00 pm, she is going to purchase tickets for a movie.

Page 67

A began, threw, doesn't, rang, fell, could, flew, broke, came, gave

Page 68

B 1. does 2. Do 3. do 4. do
5. does 6. does 7. does 8. do

C is, am, are, are, is, am, is, are, am, am, are

Page 69

D 1. are 2. has 3. talks
4. is 5. is 6. was, were
7. is 8. are

E 1. Our class includes several students from other countries.
2. Neither Susan nor Farah belongs to the Red Cross Club.
3. The player was sent off for rough play.
4. Everyone at the party was having fun.

Page 70

A 2. You must not fish in the National Park.
3. You must not camp in the National Park.
4. You must not litter in the National Park.
5. You must not feed the monkeys in the National Park.
6. You must not pick the flowers in the National Park.

B Answers may vary.

Page 71

C *Suggested answers*:
2. Sharon should not cross the road without looking. She ought to use the pedestrian crossing.
3. Tom should not be sitting down. He ought to offer the old man his seat.
4. The boys should not be playing there. They ought to go to the park.

Page 72

D *Suggested answers*:
2. John's father ought to stop smoking.
He shouldn't smoke.
He ought to give up smoking.
3. May ought to study harder.
She shouldn't play video games all the time.
She ought to read more.

 ISBN 978-81-8477-748-2

4. Tom ought to wait like everyone else.
   He shouldn't push other children in the queue.
   He ought to think about other people and take turns.
5. John ought to visit her every day.
   John shouldn't just play with his friends.
   John ought to help her clean her flat.

Page 73

E Answers may vary.

Page 74

A 1. ✗ 2. ✓ 3. ✓ 4. ✓
5. ✗ 6. ✗ 7. ✓ 8. ✓
9. ✗ 10. ✗ 11. ✓ 12. ✓

B *Suggested answers:*
1. The whole class went to the zoo.
2. We ate our lunch in the park.
3. There are many people jogging in the park.
4. I met my friends at the concert.
5. We can start when you are ready.

Page 75

C

	Subject	Predicate
2.	Cats	like fish
3.	Her hair	is black
4.	Birds	have feathers
5.	The baby	is sleeping in the cot
6.	Aunt Sarah	sent me a postcard
7.	Jenny's mother	scolded her
8.	Everyone	knows that
9.	None of us	heard the telephone ringing
10.	She	wrote a poem about the cat

Page 76

D

Subject	Verb	Object
2. Mary	is sharpening	her pencil
3. This machine	makes	a lot of noise
4. They	are playing	table tennis
5. He	was repairing	the telephone
6. Susan	likes	singing
7. A barber	cuts	hair
8. The author	wrote	an animal story
9. Everyone	enjoyed	the show
10. Dad	is reading	a magazine

Page 77

E

	Direct Object	*Indirect Object*
2.	some milk	baby
3.	minutes	children
4.	a letter	girl
5.	a song	us
6.	the way	tourist
7.	her seat	old lady
8.	driving	him
9.	the story of early Singapore	us
10.	some stamps	Peter
11.	a glass of milk	me
12.	his report card	Tom
13.	her wedding photos	friends
14.	what he saw	policeman
15.	a gift	staff member

Page 78

A Answers may vary.

Page 79

B 1. armchair 2. musicians
3. life story 4. lady
5. bird 6. afternoon
7. track 8. roar

C

	how	where	when
1. fought	✓		
2. get		✓	
3. came			✓
4. resting		✓	
5. bowed	✓		
6. see			✓
7. drove		✓	
8. wrote	✓		
9. jumped		✓	
10.	sings		✓

Page 80

D 2. fiery 3. fearsome
4. soared 5. menacingly
6. over the hills

E Teacher check.

Page 81

F 2. a statement 3. a question
4. an exclamation 5. an imperative
6. an imperative 7. a question
8. an exclamation 9. a statement
10. a question 11. an imperative
12. an exclamation 13. a question
14. a statement 15. an imperative

Page 82

A Answers may vary.

Page 83

B 2. Yes, plants grow in the desert.
No, plants don't grow in the desert.
3. Yes, I slept well last night.
No, I didn't sleep well last night.
4. Yes, my mother likes strawberries.
No, my mother doesn't like strawberries.

C 2. Yes, John has handed in his homework.
No, John hasn't handed in his homework.
3. Yes, the postman has delivered the mail.
No, the postman hasn't delivered the mail.
4. Yes, I have read some Harry Potter stories.
No, I haven't read any Harry Potter stories.

Page 84

D *Underlined question words*:
What, what, Who, What, Where, When, why, Which, How

Page 85

E 1. Why 2. When
3. Where/How/When 4. When/Why
5. When, where 6. Why
7. Why 8. How
9. Where 10. Why
11. How/When 12. How

F 1. Who 2. What 3. Who
4. Whose 5. What 6. Which
7. Which 8. Who 9. What
10. What 11. What 12. whom
13. Who 14. Whose 15. Which

Page 86

A 2. We tried really hard but did not win.
3. I might go by train or go by bus.
4. She likes the watch but has no money to buy it.
5. The Prince was tall and handsome.
6. Do your homework or you will not watch TV tonight.
7. John drew a horse as carefully as he could but it looked like a donkey.
8. The lamp was switched off and Jane was soon asleep.

Page 87

B and, or, but, and, and, but.

C Answers may vary.

Page 88

D Ever since he was a small boy, David has been helping his mother. Before he goes to school, David helps his mother tidy the apartment. First, he cleans his own room. After he has cleaned his room, he begins sweeping the kitchen. Then he washes the breakfast dishes. Finally, he tidies his desk and puts his dirty clothes in the laundry basket.

Page 89

E 1. because, and 2. Because
3. Although 4. but, when
5. First, Then, After, so

Page 90

A 1. Wading birds have long legs. Ducks have short legs.
2. Helen wants to be a teacher. Her mother is a lawyer.
3. Chinatown has lots of Chinese restaurants. There are also lots of Western restaurants there.
4. Dr Smith works in the National Eye Hostipal. He drives to work every morning.
5. In countries like China and Japan, winter starts from December and ends in February. In Australia, the seasons are opposite to those in China and Japan.

B 1. ...again. 2. ...lesson.
3. ...live? 4. ...answer?
5. ...me? 6. ...have?
7. ...meal. 8. ...lived.

Page 91

C *Suggested answers*:
1. How old is your grandmother?
2. When does this store open?
3. Where has John gone to?/Where is John?
4. What kinqds of books do you like?
5. What is your favourite sport?
6. Who is your best friend?

D *Suggested answers:*
1. In my school bag, I have some books, a lunch box and a pencil case.
2. On the mat, I can see a pinic basket, some sandwiches, some fruit, some drinks, some plates, some forks, spoons and knives.
3. In the playground, there are a slide, some swings and a see-saw.

Page 92

E 1. The Sun has nine planets. They are Mercury, Venus, Earth, Mars, Jupiter, Satum, Uranus, Neptune and Pluto. Mercury is the smallest planet and Jupiter is the largest.
2. A long time ago, there was a Greek storyteller whose name was Aesop. He told lots of stories called fables. Fables are stories with a moral. A moral is a piece of good advice about how to behave.
3. My brother and I went to Mark's birthday party on Saturday. Everyone had a good time. Mark had eight candles on his cake and everyone sang the Happy Birthday song when he blew them out.

 ISBN 978-81-8477-748-2